3HAG WAY

The **Strategic Execution System** that ensures your strategy is not a Wild-Ass-Guess!

D1534323

SHANNON BYRNE SUSKO

Foreword by Kaihan Krippendorff

Library of Congress Control Number: 2018938871

ISBN Paperback: 978-1-947368-79-8
ISBN eBook: 978-1-947368-80-4

Cover Design: Zeljka Kojic
Interior Design: Ghislain Viau

In memory of my Dad, E. Michael Byrne, who always told me
when growing my first company to make sure I take time
to stop and smell the flowers. The 3HAG WAY sure helped me
to do this! *Thanks Dad! Miss you every day!*

Table of Contents

"Strategy without tactics is the slowest route to victory. Tactics without strategy is the noise before defeat."

—*Sun Tzu*

Foreword

by Kaihan Krippendorff

Here is the problem with most business books: they focus on the easy part. They pick up their stories of Apple or Google or Starbucks after luck has struck. In their hindsight retelling of how Steve Jobs discovered design, how Larry Page and Sergey Brin figured out page-ranking, or how Howard Schultz realized Americans wanted to drink coffee, they focus on what happens *after* the birth of insights that propel breakthrough growth.

In their haste to get to the entertaining parts of their stories, they gloss over the long, agonizing slog these founders had to endure to get there.

In 1970, a team of college students from the University of Pennsylvania decided to take a leap. As a class assignment, they had written a business plan for a retail store that would sell anything college students wanted but couldn't find at shops near campus. Today Urban Outfitters is one of the most successful retail chains in the US: with $3.5 billion in revenue, the retailer consistently grows faster and produces higher profit margins than its peers. Competitors struggle to match their growth strategy, which relies on hard-to-copy factors like culture, uncommon hiring practices, and entrepreneurial processes that run counter to most retailers' affinities for efficiency and simplicity.

But Urban Outfitters struggled until around 1980, when, after a decade of trial and error, it hit upon its formula for success. After ten years of pushing for 10–15 percent growth each year, suddenly the company started growing at 40–50 percent annually.

In 1974, four years after the Urban Outfitters team took their entrepreneurial leap, two Steves, Jobs and Wozniak, decided to start building computers. Today their company, Apple, is the most valuable and one of the most admired beacons of innovation, with over $230 billion in revenue. But the story typically told about Apple overlooks that the company averaged just 3 percent growth until 2003, when something magical happened. The company suddenly accelerated, clocking nearly 40 percent annual growth for the next ten years.

Most companies endure long periods of tepid growth before they stumble upon a formula that works. Urban Outfitters took a decade to get to its scaling point; Apple took three decades.

What happens during those long slogs in search of growth? A lot of wild-ass guesses, misses, and learning.

After returning from a trip to Italy in 1984, Schultz convinced his employer, Starbucks, to test out a new coffeehouse concept. A few years later he acquired the company, and he made tons of mistakes. Customers complained about menus written in Italian, and about having to listen to opera music. Baristas hated the bow ties. Stores had no chairs. But he learned along the way, and once he figured out his strategic formula, Starbucks' revenue and store-count suddenly surged.

The slog toward growth can be demoralizing. After just a year of trying to build Google, Page was ready to give up his control of the company in his search for growth. He offered to sell the company to Excite for $1 million and work there for seven months before returning to Stanford in the fall. When Excite turned him down, he dropped the price to $700,000. Luckily for him, Excite's leadership still declined, which forced Page and Brin to embark on their search for growth on their own.

In *3HAG Way*, Shannon Susko offers a step-by-step process to shorten the time it takes to reach your scaling point. Her methodology shows you how to stop guessing, and thereby find a shortcut to growth.

I've known Shannon for years. I was drawn to her, as many are, by her uncommon accomplishments: She has launched two companies and scaled four businesses with two very successful exits—the second exit exponentially better than the first. These exits were less than six years apart, and the time between the founding and selling of her second company was just three years and three months. In 2011 Shannon was named Dealmaker of the Year by BIV/ACG in Vancouver for her sale of Subservo, and the deal itself was recognized as one of the top three mid-market deals on Wall Street that year.

That track record alone puts Shannon in the top echelon of founders that entrepreneurs should want to learn from. But what makes her truly stand out is her talent for synthesizing knowledge into tools you can immediately apply. While many successful business leaders base their knowledge on their experience, Shannon also devises her methodologies by standing on the shoulders of giants. She reads more business books, attends more conferences, and draws knowledge from more business thinkers than anyone I know. She leverages what works from leading business experts like Jim Collins, Michael Porter, Renée Mauborgne, W. Chan Kim, Verne Harnish, Geoffrey Moore, Alexander Osterwalder, and even my own work, refines it through application in her businesses, and infuses her personal experience. She doesn't try to reinvent the wheel, nor does she burden you with unproven fluff.

The result is a system that may at first seem complex, but reveals itself as elegant once you step into it. Her framework will help you shorten the path to growth by applying a scientific approach that removes much of the guesswork from your search for that path. In essence, Shannon offers a methodology to engineer the luck that many business owners blindly pray for.

Had Page or Brin or Jobs or Wozniak or the Urban Outfitters team followed the 3HAG strategic execution system, their companies they founded might be five years ahead of where they are now, or even more. Collectively, at their current growth rates, this would equate to nearly $170 billion in new revenue. Imagine what it might do for you.

Kaihan Krippendorff
Founder and CEO of Outthinker, author of Outthink the Competition, top-choice keynote speaker and consultant on business strategy, innovation, growth, creativity and leadership.

Acknowledgements

I would like to express my sincere gratitude to the many people who saw me through this book.

I would like to thank the BusinessGhost team, especially Michael Levin, Bryan Gage, Barbara Richter, Jenny Sommerfeld, and Rebecca Frost, for enabling me to publish this book.

Thank you to Kaihan Krippendorff for his thought leadership on strategy. His work has made me a better coach and my clients more strategic thinkers through his Outthinker Methodology.

I would like to thank my team at www.shannonsusko.com, Hailey Manchee, Devon Brusse, and Rachel Byrne, for their incredible patience throughout this process, and for always being available to support me when I needed it—no matter what day or time.

Thanks to the Metronome Growth Systems team—especially my co-founding partners, Benoit Bourget and Paul Rempel—for their incredible insight, feedback, and expertise in creating an online platform that will benefit entrepreneurs, leaders and their teams worldwide. This platform is significant in making visible your strategic execution system and aligning leaders and their teams to reach their 3HAG and then their BHAG!

Thanks to ACETECH—Kathy Troupe and Simon Cloutier—for their unwavering support of me over the last twenty years, first as a growing CEO and now as a growth company thought leader and coach. Thanks for offering your Growth Strategy Program to your members based on my first book, *The Metronome Effect*, and for your unwavering commitment to CEOs and leaders who want to grow their companies and better their communities.

Keith Cupp and his team at Gazelles International Coaches have been instrumental in confirming the effectiveness of the 3HAG WAY! Many thanks to all the GIC coaches who learned this methodology early on and achieved incredible results with their clients. These results and their feedback encouraged me to write this book and share this methodology. Thank you to the first coach to use the methodology—Rich Manders of Freescale Coaching Systems.

Thanks to Verne Harnish for supporting me through my journey with his book *Mastering the Rockefeller Habits* and challenging me to find my metronome. This experience helped drive me and my team to find the practical strategic execution system outlined in the 3HAG WAY.

Thanks to all the thought leaders mentioned throughout this book. Their thoughtful work, experience, and wisdom challenged me to find practical tools my team and my clients can use every day.

I would like to thank the Paradata team for their never-ending faith and support for my nontraditional methods, and for their commitment to the process.

I must also thank my co-founding Subserveo partner, Mike Hagerman, for his enthusiastic encouragement and unwavering belief in this process. And a big thank you to the Subserveo team for proving the value of the 3HAG methodology.

Above all I want to thank my husband, Sko (Chris Susko), and my three children, Cain, Matthew, and Embyr-Lee, who supported and encouraged me in spite of the time it took me away from them. Love you to the mountains and back and beyond!

Last but not least, I beg the forgiveness of all those who have been with me over the years whose names I have failed to mention.

Invitation

The best way to predict your future is to create it.
—Peter F. Drucker

N o one should have to go through what I went through.

In the 1990s, I was working a hundred hours a week at the first company I cofounded, Paradata. And despite the fact that I was putting in those inhumanely long hours, things were not going well. Actually, things were going poorly—quite poorly. I'll explain more about Paradata in the chapters ahead, and how we ultimately thrived despite finding ourselves between a rock and a hard place. For now, though, all you need to know is that this book is *an invitation*. Yes, you read that right: This book is an invitation. It's an invitation to sidestep the excruciating process that I went through with Paradata and avoid the painful, traditional business-planning process, and to choose, instead, a reliable, repeatable Strategic Execution System that will put your company squarely on track to meet its goal—from day one.

That Strategic Execution System is called the 3HAG: your "3 Year Highly Achievable Goal." The House Diagram below shows where the 3HAG fits into the six systems that exist in every business: Cultural System, Team Cohesive System, Human System, Execution System, Cash System, and Strategy System. At Paradata we used the term *system* because once you start this framework, you and your team will forever evolve it and make it your own.

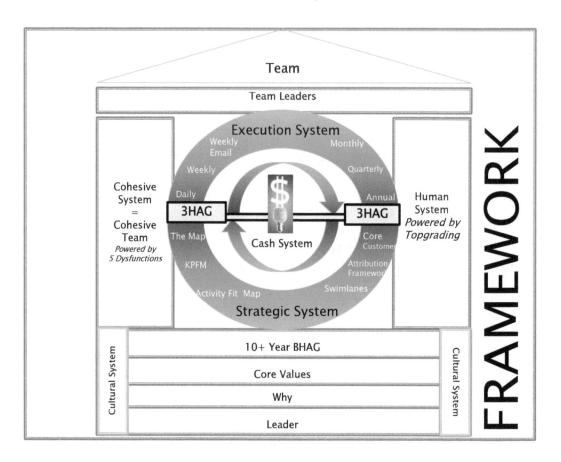

In the pages ahead, I will reveal all the details of the 3HAG, and I will explain exactly why it's crucial that your company use a Strategic Execution System that connects its weekly, monthly, quarterly, annual, near-term, and long-term goals. That Strategic Execution System is the 3HAG. Soon, the 3HAG framework will act as your company's road map for aligning your daily actions and near-term execution with your company's long-term goal—or, to use the term coined by Jim Collins, your Big Hairy Audacious Goal (BHAG).[1] Indeed, your long-term goal should drive your day-to-day activities.

1 Jim Collins and Jerry I. Porras, *Built to Last: Successful Habits of Visionary Companies* (New York: Harper Business, 1994).

While achieving such alignment between your BHAG and day-to-day actions may sound like a pipe dream, you can and will do it by developing your 3HAG. The 3HAG will deliver clarity about exactly what you and your team need to do—month over month, quarter over quarter, and year over year—to meet your goals.

That sounds like a tall order, but I can tell you that I have intensively tested the 3HAG with my own companies. In fact, I ended up betting my position as CEO on this framework, and it paid off in a big way. At Paradata, facing a tough situation, we *created* the 3HAG in order to save our company. We followed a specific set of strategic guidelines—which you're about to receive in full—and built a Strategic Execution System based on a 3 year time frame aligned to our 10-to-30-year goal. Paradata grew, and so did our confidence.

The 3HAG framework worked so well, in fact, that I used it at my second company, Subserveo, which became one of the fastest-growing companies and top exits in North America for midsize companies in 2011.

At that time I didn't realize that what we were doing with our 3HAG was so different from what other CEOs were doing to develop and grow *their* companies. In fact, I eventually learned that the 3HAG is the opposite of what many CEOs do. When I ultimately became a coach, after selling Subserveo, I discovered that many companies are far from having a clear strategy and 10-to-30-year goal that the whole team is working toward. And many don't have a clear strategy at all. In many cases, CEOs are reluctant even to share their strategy with their team members. In other cases, the strategy is so complex that it takes twenty minutes to explain. Unfortunately, those CEOs are likely to have as hard a time as I had during Paradata's early years.

But that doesn't have to be you. With your 3HAG in place, your company can accelerate toward growth—be focused, have fun with your team, and realize the freedom you are striving for.

In January 2016, I cofounded my third company, Metronome Growth Systems, a cloud-based platform that supports CEOs and coaches of high-growth companies who are committed to this framework. This book preaches what I practiced as a CEO and what I now communicate as a coach to CEOs and in my workshops around the world. After hosting hundreds of strategy-focused workshops, I figured it was time to write down the 3HAG in its entirety, so everyone could benefit from this predictable growth framework.

I became a coach with the express purpose of helping CEOs reach strategic clarity to execute the growth of their businesses and realize their goals. That's why this book is specifically for CEOs, executives, their coaches, and anyone in a position to grow a business. And while you may be wondering if the strategies outlined in this book will work for *your* company, I can tell you that I've coached CEOs at companies with 10 to 100 to 1,000+ team members. This framework is scalable, and it works.

In the pages ahead you'll find step-by-step instructions on how to create a focused, actionable, Strategic Execution System that will align your priorities to your BHAG (10-to-30-year goal), your 3HAG (3 Year Highly Achievable Goal), your 1HAG (1 Year Highly Achievable Goal—your Annual Plan), and the next ninety days. The Core Purpose of this book is to have a positive impact on CEOs, their leadership teams, their families, their companies, and the communities they live in. This is what I realized with my companies.

Whether you run a team of 10, 100, or 1,000+, the tools and framework in this book will help you articulate your company's core strategy and execute it with confidence. We're going to tackle each step of the Strategic Execution System in bite-size pieces, so that you'll know exactly how and why each step is critical to achieving your goal—your *3HAG*.

Ready? Let's get started.

Chapter 1

Are You Driving Your Business or Just Driving Around the Block?

Good is the enemy of great. And that is one of the key reasons
why we have so little that becomes great.
—Jim Collins, *Good to Great*

n 1995 I cofounded my first company, Paradata, with a really good idea, a half-baked strategy, and what I called a "wild-ass-guess" about where we were headed. We told everyone that we were going somewhere big. That's what we sold to the venture capitalists.

It was 1995: the edge of the internet bubble years. We had successfully raised venture capital on that wild-ass-guess of a business plan that stated our intention to build a global GIS data encryption platform that included payment processing. We successfully sold the venture capitalists on this Big Hairy Audacious Goal (BHAG), even though we didn't have a detailed plan to back it up. The business plan contained few real, solid details about where we were headed or when and how we were going to get there. It was 1995 and easy to raise money on just a good idea.

I sure don't recommend this approach—and as you'll see, the mistakes we made, and how we overcame them, are the reason I'm writing this book. I don't want anyone to be as desperate as we were to grow a company and reach our goals. I want you to know where you are going and how you are going to get there with confidence. As leaders, we bet our lives, our savings, and our investors' capital. I want you to be great at predicting your company's future.

At Paradata, our investors quickly lost patience each time we pivoted, and the team was tired of running hard without the success we expected. By 1997, all stakeholders had run out of patience entirely. We were facing a do-or-die situation. That is when we made our final pivot, to become a leading global payment processor. And with this pivot we had to get clear on exactly where we were headed. We either had to clearly map out where we were going or stop wasting people's time and money.

It was only when faced with this existential threat that our newly pivoted payment-processing company finally did what we should have done at the very beginning.

To develop the clarity we needed in order to grow our company into what we wanted it to be, we began to map out our strategy. Our first few business plans were traditional and full of wild-ass-guesses; in this new plan we mapped out quarter over quarter for twelve quarters and aligned it to our 10-to-30-year goal. That is, this plan was different. This time, we weren't guessing. This time we not only did the work of analyzing our place in the market, we set our 3 Year Highly Achievable Goal aligned to our strategy and to our 10-to-30-year goal, and then mapped out exactly how we were going to achieve all of that, from the present day to 36 months away.

Since we knew there were plenty of experts and thought leaders who had created strategic and growth frameworks to help businesses grow, we didn't try to reinvent the wheel by developing a framework from scratch. Rather, we drew on a wealth of different frameworks that had already been developed and proven by some of the greatest minds in business. We wanted to create a practical framework that could be implemented even in a high-growth company. By using a mix of a number of different tools in our planning process, we actually ended up creating a new, repeatable, practical strategic framework that drew on wisdom from the business thought leaders of our time (and we are still adding tools that are applicable today). What we created became the 3 Year Highly Achievable Goal (3HAG) framework, which has now helped hundreds of businesses from start-up to midsize to multinational effectively and visibly map their success and realize it while also reducing their risk. It sounds amazing—and it is. The 3HAG must be led by a committed and deliberate leadership team that wants to achieve its goals—and wants to put the effort in to do so.

The 3HAG framework became our guide. It was the tool we used to help us define our unique and valuable market position. It was the tool we used to devise our twelve quarter-over-quarter plan. And it was the tool we used to follow through on the plan, month over month, quarter over quarter, and year over year, in order to actually meet our 3 Year Highly Achievable Goal on time and right on the numbers.

In 1998, we had faced a group of very impatient investors. By 2006, thanks to 3HAG, Paradata had achieved its goals, and we successfully sold the company. That's how powerful the 3HAG is.

The 3HAG framework allowed us to hit an absolute home run when we launched our second company, Subserveo. In just three years after launching Subserveo, we met our first 3HAG, and we were highly valued because of it. Three months later, we sold the company for a massive return to investors in the worst market in a hundred years. How did we build Subserveo into such an unqualified success in such a short time frame? By using the 3HAG to map out exactly where this new company was headed and then executing on the specific quarter-over-quarter plan. In fact, when the company that would eventually acquire Subserveo first looked at our One-Page Strategic Plan—a tool that you'll read about shortly—they saw that, in our very first quarter of business, we had predicted exactly where we were going to be in *quarter twelve*, three years out. That's right: we forecasted where we were going to be in three years, and then we hit those numbers. The company's value increased based on our ability to predict the future with confidence.

The company that eventually bought Subserveo was totally blown away by this. They saw that we were exactly where we said we would be. And they could hardly believe that such a young company had applied such a mature planning process to predict its position three years in the future—and had then marched toward its goals, quarter over quarter, for twelve quarters. Our line of progress toward our 3HAG was not absolutely straight, of course, but our progress was always forward, and we were constantly discussing and evolving with the Subserveo team quarter over quarter—so that by quarter twelve, we were on the numbers.

What's unfortunate is how unusual this example is. Most companies operate the way that Paradata did in its first couple of years: on a wild-ass-guess and without any clearly mapped-out plan. I am not saying that all companies are like this, but very few companies operate like Subserveo, following a clear road map, quarter over quarter, laid out specifically for twelve quarters.

But Subserveo doesn't have to be so unusual. On the contrary, Subserveo's march to success should be standard business protocol. If companies took the time to plot out their strategy beyond four quarters and align their next twelve quarters with their near-term and long-term goals—rather than just hoping that their current activities would yield success—then far more businesses would confidently succeed, have fun doing it, and realize their goals.

If that's what you want to do, keep reading.

The Undeniable Importance of the 3HAG

After working with hundreds of companies over the past decade, I've heard every excuse under the sun for why companies can't pull together a simple and clear 3HAG.

"Our business is going to change so quickly in the next three weeks—let alone three years—there's no way we can plan for it!"

"It's too hard!"

"What's the big deal about a 3-year plan anyway?" (I'll answer that question in a moment.)

"I can't do a 3-year plan—I'm too busy putting out fires!"

When you're just starting out, or even if you have been in business a long time, it can be overwhelming to sit down and plan where your company is going. I get that, because I felt the same anxiety at Paradata and in some of the bigger companies I was acquired into. Who has time to strategize when you're focused on executing? Don't we have a good strategy we developed five years ago?

But the problem is that without a solid plan that is evolving as the market you are playing in evolves, you're unlikely to grow (and you're really likely not to achieve your goals). As a coach, I now work with many companies that excel at executing—but they're not growing. In many of these cases the leadership team doesn't have a clear picture or cannot articulate where the company fits in the larger marketplace. And rather than executing a plan based on where they'd like to be three years from now, they end up executing based on where they've always been and in response to competitors' actions. A few big names—Kodak, Blockbuster—and thousands of others have gone out of business with this approach.

Operating a business without an evolving strategy is like driving a bus around the block. You drive up to a stop sign, you flip on your blinker, and you turn right. At the next stop sign, you flip on your blinker and turn right again. At the next stop sign, same thing. Nothing changes. If you don't have an evolving growth strategy, then you and your team are just driving around the block. You may be doing very well, but you are not going anywhere.

If you actually loaded your whole team onto a bus, the first question you would get is, "Where are we going?" and then someone would ask, "How long will it take?" and then someone else would have to ask, "Do we have enough gas to get there?" And then, "What is our first stop?"

Those are excellent questions, and you and your team should be able to answer them. And by developing your 3HAG, you *will* answer them. Then you will drive to exactly where you say you're going, in the amount of time you say it will take to get there and with the resources required.

Before we go any further, let's address the common question that I hear from CEOs: *What's the big deal about creating a 3HAG? Why do you need a 3 Year Highly Achievable Goal in order to succeed?* Perhaps you agree that you need a clear and simple strategy—but why three years? Why not five years?

Because three years is where the near term and the long term meet. If you're like many CEOs, right now you may already have a five-year plan or even a ten-year plan stashed away somewhere, because most people understand the value of setting long-term goals. Those long-term goals are more or less an aspirational image for where you want to land in the future. I would put five-year planning into this "long-range" category. A five-year plan may actually be easier to write than a three-year plan; it's easier to write precisely because it's more of a

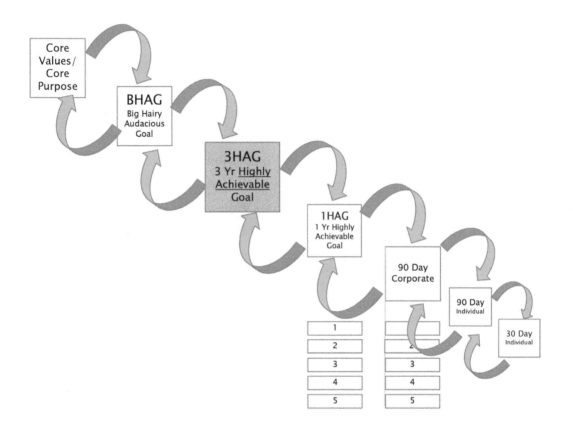

guess than a plan—or, as I like to call it, your 5 Year Wild-Ass-Guess. Five years is too far out to really know what you'll be doing.

But three years isn't. Three years is where your near-term work meets your long-term goal. Your 3HAG is your clear and visible map for the near term. The beauty of the 3HAG, as a matter of fact, is that it's so close you can reach out and touch it—if you take the time to plan with your team.

Note, though, that I'm not recommending you develop your 3HAG *instead of* a long-term goal. You've got to do both: you need a 3HAG *plus* a long-term goal. This long-term goal is your 10-to-30-year goal, or what Jim Collins refers to as your Big Hairy Audacious Goal (BHAG).

In a moment we'll talk about setting your BHAG. For now, what's important is that you understand the significance of the 3HAG plus the BHAG: Your 3HAG will serve as a twelve-quarter-by-quarter framework for the next thirty-six months of forward movement toward your BHAG. Three years, thirty-six months, or twelve quarters—however you look at it—that time frame allows you to get into the nitty-gritty details of strategic execution with your leadership team, and over time, your whole team. You create the Strategic Execution System road map, discuss it, write it down, and draw it out in pictures (Strategic Pictures—which we will define later), so everyone *sees* where you're going, and then you *execute while never ceasing to evolve the Strategic Execution System road map as things continuously change around your company.*

Once you have this step-by-step guide in place, you'll find that you have greater confidence in each action you take. You'll be following a clear road map rather than just reacting to competitors. That road map builds confidence. And you'll find that your confidence increases over time.

Every entrepreneur will tell you that building a business is an iterative process. You're like an athlete training by running around a track. On the first few laps you may find that you're not in great shape, but as you take one lap after another, your fitness builds, and your confidence builds along with it. You keep getting better and better. You start to ace the planning process. You're adding to your road map. You're building your business. You're back in the planning room—but now you know exactly what you need to cover in your meetings. It's the same agenda, you work with your team, you map out your goals, and then you get right back to building and growing.

Then you repeat again: create, discuss, write it down, draw or evolve the pictures to build your confidence, and *execute again.*

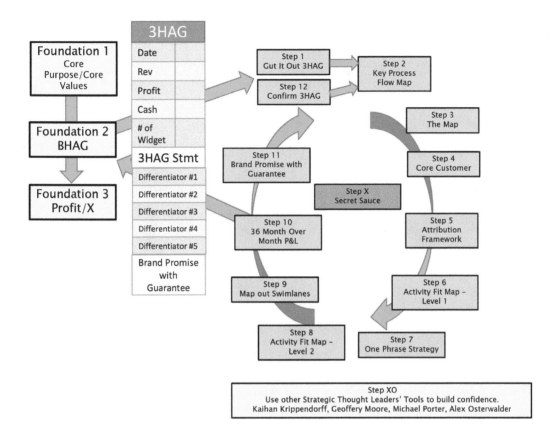

What this book explains is a *repeatable* Strategic Execution System. Once you've got the hang of the 3HAG, you'll wonder how you ever got along without it.

CHAPTER TAKEAWAYS

✔ Once you've developed your 3 Year Highly Achievable Goal and started executing on a quarter-by-quarter basis, you'll speed toward success.

Chapter 2
Foundation for Growth

Growth is never by mere chance;
it is the result of forces working together.
—James Cash Penney

Every company needs to clearly understand its foundation, its reason for being. Every team needs to understand why it exists and what behaviors are acceptable, and to believe in its long-term goal. These fundamental components are what make up a team's Cultural System.

Your team's Cultural System represents your corporate team's culture. If your corporate culture isn't solid on its values, and if your team doesn't understand and buy into the company's reason for existing, then strategic planning will not right the ship. Team culture trumps strategy.

In other words, your company must have a strong foundation before you build your Strategic Execution System. I've seen plenty of CEOs who would rather put on blinders and avoid this issue forever, but I'm afraid that's not an option. If your company lacks clarity about core values, then you'll keep driving around the block instead of driving forward.

So before you can create the 3HAG that will deliver the growth you're seeking, your company's Core Purpose and core values must be strong, clear, and embraced by the whole team.

Ask yourself—and answer honestly—*are your Core Purpose, core values, and 10-to-30-year goal strong, clear, and known by all on your team?* If not, take the time to build your Foundation for Growth. (And even if they are, take some time to ensure they are really solid and clear.)

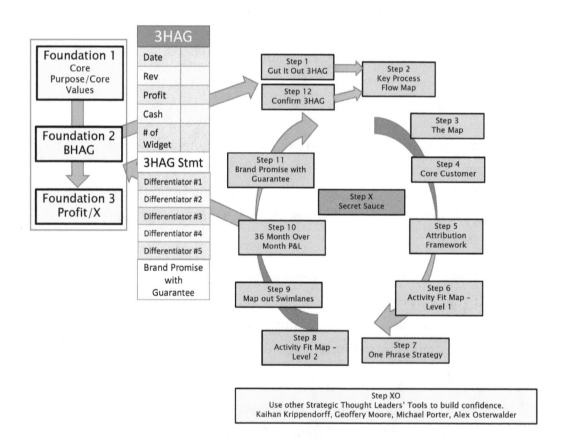

Foundation 1—Core Purpose and Core Values

A. **Core Purpose: Why does this organization exist?** The answer may be very simple, but it's essential that everyone knows the big "why." Why does this company exist in the first place? If the founder is in the room, have him or her simply answer why the company was started and give a reason for its existence. This could be the Core Purpose. At Paradata, we determined that our Core Purpose was "To create an organization that others would value, and to create a great place to work." Simple. We were building a company to be sold in fewer than five years at the highest valuation possible and have fun doing it. Other Core Purpose examples include "Escape" (Starbucks) and "Happy" (Disney).

If the Core Purpose of the company has evolved from the reason the founder(s) started the company, follow this process:

a. With your leadership team, ask the simple question: "Core Purpose: Why does this organization exist?"

b. Before any answers are verbalized, give each leader a 2 × 3 pad of sticky notes and ask them to write down their answer.

c. When all leaders have written their answers, have each leader share their answer and post it on a whiteboard or easel, grouping answers that are similar.

d. Once all have presented their answers, look at them and discuss what the Core Purpose of the organization should be.

e. This may end up in draft form, or you can ask a volunteer to take a picture of the sticky notes to write a Core Purpose to bring to the next meeting.

B. **Core values: What are the consistent, accepted behaviors of your team members?** Most companies already have core values, which just need to be discovered, articulated, and clearly communicated and acknowledged. These core values represent the behaviors of the team members and are not the external corporate/brand core values. These are the core values that you are evaluating and hiring on. Core values are in a person; they cannot be coached and are hard to identify in a candidate when hiring. This is who a person is. The team must understand its team's core values before even considering hiring someone—you need to know what you represent before you bring in someone new. That way, you'll have a better sense of whether your new hire also represents your core values.

A great tool to help discover your team's core values is Jim Collins's "Mars Group." This tool asks you and your team to recreate the very best attributes of your organizational team on another planet and there are only five seats on the rocket ship. Who do you send to be the best example of your team's attributes? This tool will help you discover and confirm your core values, and I highly recommend that you do this with your team. You can download this tool at http://www.jimcollins.com/tools/vision-framework.pdf.

At Paradata, Subserveo, and Metronome Growth Systems (all the companies I cofounded), our core values were/are "Happy, Humble, Hungry."

Core Value	One Phrase Description
Happy	Happy to come to work, Happy to go home
Hungry	Hungry enough to want to make a difference every day
Humble	Humble enough to want to learn every day

That meant every one of our team members was happy to come to work and happy to leave at the end of the day, hungry enough to make a difference every day, and humble enough to want to learn something new every day. Our goal was to ensure that no ball hit the floor, regardless of the position you were in on the team.

A few examples of other core values common at other businesses include the following:

SquareSpace[1]
Purpose: Giving voice to ideas.
Values:

- Be your own customer
- Empower individuals
- Design is not a luxury
- Good work takes time
- Optimize toward ideals
- Simplify

Learn more about the values at Squarespace: http://www.squarespace.com/about/values

Atlassian[1]
Purpose: To unleash the potential in every team and help advance humanity through the power of software.
Values:

- Open company, no bullshit
- Build with heart and balance
- Don't #@!% the customer
- Play as a team
- Be the change you seek

Learn more about the values at Atlassian: https://www.atlassian.com/company/careers

So what are your company's core values? Are they clear and known? Do you hire and fire on these core values? Why is this important to your 3HAG? If everyone on the team has the same core values and believes in the Core Purpose and your long-term goal, it will be much easier to get everyone rowing together in the direction you want to

---

1 Source: https://yscouts.com/culture-2/top-10-core-values -medium-workplaces/

go with less energy. Take the time now to complete the Mars Group exercise created by Jim Collins.

Foundation 2—BHAG

Big Hairy Audacious Goal (BHAG): What do you want your company to be in ten to thirty years' time? I have asked thousands of CEOs if they have a 10-to-30-year goal, and fewer than 40 percent of them do, which has been a real eye opener for me as a coach and speaker. Their excuse is that it's too far away and they have no idea what the market will be doing by that time. Or they tell me there's no way they'll still be at the company by that time (but that's even *more* of a reason to create a 10-to-30-year goal for the company). Your BHAG should paint a picture of what the company is going to be/accomplish in ten to thirty years. While a BHAG doesn't need to be highly specific, it does need to show a clear endgame. This is vital for creating clarity about where the "bus" is going to end up. It guides the team to make good decisions each day—decisions that are aligned with the BHAG.

Indeed, when it comes to your BHAG, it's not about the how, it's about the *what*. At Paradata, our BHAG was to become the world's leading global payment provider. We deliberately wrote this BHAG with no numbers. None. And I highly recommend you don't use numbers, either. We didn't specify that we wanted Paradata to become a $100 million business, or that we wanted to have 10,000 merchant customers. We did, however, measure our BHAG—this 10-to-30-year goal—by measuring our Profit/X—which, in the case of Paradata, was Profit/Merchant (see the next section for an explanation of Profit/X). And once you establish your BHAG with your team, I recommend painting a picture of this for all to see and remember. The Painted Picture concept is described in Cameron Herold's book *Double Double*. You can download an adapted version from my website, http://www.shannonsusko.com/.

So, now is the time to specify your BHAG. Even if you have one, I highly recommend this process:

a. With your leadership team, ask the question, "What is the 10-to-30-year goal of this organization—written with no numbers?"

b. Before any answers are verbalized, give each leader a 2 × 3 pad of sticky notes and ask them to write down their answer.

c. When all leaders have written their answers, have each one share their answer and post it on a whiteboard or easel, grouping answers that are similar.

d. Once all have presented their answers, look at those answers and discuss what the BHAG—the 10-to-30-year goal of the organization—should be.

e. This might end up in draft form, or you can ask a volunteer to take a picture of the sticky notes to write a BHAG to bring to the next meeting.

Foundation 3—Profit/X

What's your economic engine? How will you make money? The "Profit/X" concept was created by Jim Collins to clarify what you are passionate about, what you can be best at in the world, and how you will make money at it.[2] On his website, Collins describes it as "the economic denominator that best drives our economic engine (profit or cash flow per 'x')."[3] This is a mechanism to measure your BHAG. A lot of companies do not instantly come up with Profit/X, but as stated before, I am a big fan of gutting it out at this stage; through this process and over time it will be become clearer and clearer. Paradata's Profit/X was Profit/Merchant. We wanted to make money for every new merchant

---

2 Jim Collins, *Good to Great* (New York: William Collins, 2001).

3 Jim Collins, October 2001, accessed February 1, 2018: http://www.jimcollins.com/article_topics/articles/good-to-great.html.

and existing merchant on our platform. We were a subscription-based payment-processing business in which merchants bought subscriptions to our platform, so our core economic number was profit per *merchant*. For every merchant using our platform, we forecasted what our Profit/Merchant number was going to be in one year, three years, and ten-plus years. Not only did this number help us stay focused on our 3HAG, it helped keep us aligned with our BHAG. At its essence, Profit/X reflects both your core competencies and your plan to *make* money.

So, what is *your* Profit/X?

a. With your leadership team, ask, "What is our organization's Profit/X? What is it that we will make money on every time?"

b. Before any answers are verbalized, give each leader a 2 × 3 pad of sticky notes and ask them to write their answer.

c. When all leaders have written their answers, have each one share their answer and post it on a whiteboard or easel, grouping the answers that are similar.

d. Once all have presented their answers, look at them, and discuss what the "Profit/X" is now.

We will map out your company's Key Process Flow Chart for the present and the future—which will help us get clearer on what your X should be for this year, three years from now, and ten-plus years away. For now I am happy you will have a starting point and a point to agree or disagree on for the future.

Talking about Core Purpose, core values, BHAG, and your Profit/X is hard work. It's even harder than hammering out your strategy. But it's well worth the effort and time. Do NOT skimp on this section—it is your Foundation for Growth and everything you will do going forward to achieve your goals. So please take the time to review, confirm, or establish these three foundational ingredients. They are absolutely critical.

I am a Patrick Lencioni junkie. I've read every book he has published. Why? Because as a CEO (and now as a coach), the more I could learn about people and teams, the more successful I was. Shockingly, I spend most of my time working with teams in this area of the Cultural System as well as the Team Cohesive System and the Human System. For more information about these foundational people systems, read my first book, and explore the many resources available at http://www.shannonsusko.com/.

3HAG and Your Team

High-performing companies tend to have a strong organizational culture with core values known and embraced by all team members. When everyone on *your* team aligns with your company's core values, Core Purpose, and BHAG, you'll be on your way to success.

As you begin this process with your team, you may find that it's difficult to get team members to really talk about strategy. It will take patience on your part to create the time and structure that ultimately encourage people to start talking and strategizing.

Your goal is to create what strategic coaches commonly refer to as the "collaborative brain." In the collaborative brain, everyone works together to develop the 3HAG. Members of the group share ideas and suggestions based on their unique perspective, and that improves the overall outcome. There have been plenty of times when I've walked into a meeting as a CEO *knowing* what a strategy and plan should be—then walked out with a much better version of them. Nine brains are much better than one, as long as you're all working toward the same goal.

Creating this kind of atmosphere requires Team Accountability, in which everyone is invested in the shared goal from day one. Team Accountability is not "Did you get *xyz* done?" or "When are *you* going to complete that assignment?" It's ensuring the success of the company by being accountable to *each other for the team win.*

The recently released book *Blue Ocean Shift*, written by W. Chan Kim and Renée Mauborgne, clearly states that the third component of any Strategic Execution System is the humanness component. It was amazing to read and realize that others have recognized how important this is to achieving any Team Goal. The concept is obvious but hard to implement, and it's hard to articulate its importance. It means that the whole team needs to be inspired and confident to own and drive the Strategic Execution System—not just the CEO and/ or the leadership team. Everyone on the team needs to be aware and contribute in some way to where the company is going and how the team is going to get there. And guess what? They want to own it! Yes, it is very human to want to drive toward the goal, rather than to be told what to do to get there. They want to create, decide, and execute—with pride. We learned this squarely at Paradata and again confirmed that if we implement this Strategic Execution System founded on the Foundation for Growth—with the right people and the human component—we will achieve our 3HAG and BHAG and thus stay focused, have fun, and realize our freedom.

Such an atmosphere may sound difficult to create. The truth is that it starts with the CEO and leadership. So it's on you to learn as much as you can about high-performing teams and how to implement to become great leaders as well as coaches of this Strategic Execution System. This is not a quick fix for any team—this process can be coupled with the Strategic Execution System. They go hand in hand. The more you make sure every meeting works on the human side of the team as well as the Strategic Execution System, the stronger and more cohesive your team will grow over time. Check out http://www.shannonsusko.com/ and Patrick Lencioni's https://www.tablegroup.com/.

Access your Team Accountability by looking at the graph below and deciding where your team would be in relation to the X and Y axes.

TEAM ACCOUNTABILITY ASSESSMENT

- *No Team Accountability*—meaning that no one is accountable for the Team Goal, not even the leaders. All teams and team members are siloed and focused on their department's or team's goals only and not concerned with the broader Team Goals.

- *Leaders are accountable, and their team members are not*—meaning leaders are aware and feel accountable for the whole company's Team Goal, but their team members are still focused on their individual and departmental goals.

- *Team members are accountable for the whole company's Team Goal and their leaders are their coaches*—meaning that the whole company understands the Team Goal and is empowered, clear, and owning the Team Result. Their leaders are there to guide and coach their team members for the win. This is the ultimate goal of Team Accountability. Most teams I worked with were working from the position of *Leaders are accountable, and their team members are not* toward *Team members are accountable for the whole company's Team Goal and their leaders are their coaches.*

Team Accountability, strategy, and execution need to be eased into, and the 3HAG Strategic Execution System is a great way to do this. This process is an evolution to meld together your strategy, your execution, and your people system by using Team Accountability to the Team Goal results. I am excited to talk more about this as we progress through this framework.

Your First Lap

You've just taken your first lap around the track. You're on your way to building your 3HAG, building confidence, and building a business that will drive toward its goals rather than driving around the block.

We've talked about the importance of the 3HAG. We've tackled the Foundation for Growth—your Core Purpose, team core values, your BHAG, and your Profit/X. WOW! Now it's time to dig into strategy and your 3HAG.

CHAPTER TAKEAWAYS

✔ Foundation for Growth is the key to being able to decide on your 3HAG and execute it.

✔ Key elements of the Foundation for Growth: your Core Purpose, team core values, your BHAG, and your Profit/X. Before you can reach for growth, you've got to have the proper foundation in place.

✔ Take the time to discover, articulate, and communicate with your team about the big *Why*—why your company exists in the first place—and the behaviors that are accepted and embraced by the team.

✔ Your Big Hairy Audacious Goal (BHAG) is your 10-to-30-year vision for the company. Your BHAG, along with your Core Purpose and core values, is your Foundation for Growth.

The Strategic Execution System that Ensures Your Strategy Is Not a Wild-Ass-Guess!

✔ Profit/X is the core of your economic engine. Forecast your Profit/X for one year, three years, and ten-plus years.

✔ How you include your whole team is the key to strategy, execution, and Team Accountability to achieve the Team Goal. The human-ness component is as important as the strategy and the execution plan. These three components decrease your risk and are important to evolve together.

Chapter 3

GUT IT OUT:
Your First 3HAG

Do not wait until the conditions are perfect to begin.
Beginning makes the conditions perfect.
—Alan Cohen

L ots of people talk about strategy, but everyone seems to have a different idea of what strategy really is. I ask CEOs and leaders regularly to define the word *strategy*, and each will define it a little differently. So to be clear from the very start, I want to share with you the definition of *strategy* that we used with my teams and that I use today with all the companies I coach. We used and will use throughout this book the definition of *strategy* from Harvard Business School Professor Michael Porter's seminal book *Competitive Strategy:*[1]

Strategy describes how a company creates a unique and valuable position through a set of differentiating actions.

That's it. No fanfare, no bells or whistles, just clear, simple, and memorable: Your strategy will describe how your company has made itself *unique and valuable* in your industry through a set of differentiating actions you have decided to implement. Your business might

---

1 Michael Porter, *Competitive Strategy* (New York: The Free Press, 1980).

offer the same products as another company, but it will compete to be unique in its own dimension. The more a company competes to be unique, and not the best, the more likely it is to succeed. Whatever it is, your strategy spells out how you will position your organization to create a unique space in the marketplace. Strategy is how you're going to avoid competing on the same plane as everyone else; if you lack a strategy, then you *will* compete on the same plane as everyone else, and you will not realize your goals.

Here's a real-world example of the power of strategy. My second company, Subserveo, was a financial technology firm that provided automated, post-trade compliance service in the cloud for broker-dealers in North America. We were the last entrants into the marketplace. We had purchased the same technology that all the other companies already had. *But we sought to create a unique and valuable position by analyzing and deciding what our differentiating actions were going to be.*

We discovered that the giants in our market were competing for the large and extra-large broker-dealers and financial service companies. With that in mind, we decided to position Subserveo to focus on the small- to medium-size broker-dealers. Subserveo became the only player catering to that part of the market and to that Core Customer.

When we defined our strategy, we saw that we wanted to dominate the small- to medium-size customer marketplace. Then we mapped out the steps we would have to take to get there over the next three years. (We'll go through those steps shortly.)

Once Subserveo had launched, we dedicated year one to the small broker-dealer customers in Canada. In the second year, we went after the small- and medium-size broker-dealer customers in Canada and the United States. By our third year, our strategy had evolved and we were ready to go for the large and even extra-large customers in

North America. By then we had met our goal of leading the market for small- and medium-size customers.

Even though all of our competitors seemed to do essentially the same thing we did, we positioned ourselves to provide for the specific needs of the smaller broker-dealers first, and we did so with a long-term view in mind.

Subserveo grew fast. Surprisingly, those small- and medium-size broker-dealers represented 80 percent of the market, and it was ours for the taking. The giants in our market started trying to compete with Subserveo for the small- to medium-size broker-dealers, but they were not operationally set up to serve these broker-dealers in profitable fashion, so they retreated. That's how Subserveo won a huge market share. If we had focused on the same customers as our competition, we would have failed.

And because we focused on an underserved segment of the marketplace, after the market giants tried to compete with us and were not successful, they left us alone. That's how we established our *unique and valuable position*—by being certain about how we were going to serve our Core Customer now and in the future. We were able to grow in the marketplace until we were so large that we could compete for the largest clients. Subserveo became a contender precisely because we positioned ourselves uniquely and valuably in a place where the competition was not active.

That initial 3HAG plan included a month-over-month, quarter-over-quarter, year-over-year plan to evolve our differentiating actions and maintain our unique and valuable position for a rolling three years. We focused and analyzed, internally and externally—and as we grew, our strategy evolved to ensure we stayed on track for our 3HAG.

The 3HAG Is Born

As you read in chapter 1, things didn't initially go so smoothly in the early years of my first business, Paradata, as we weren't clear about what our strategy was. No one could articulate the strategy in a sentence or a phrase, and the whole company definitely did not know what the strategy was—few of us did. I got tired of getting up in front of the board with a wild-ass-guess of a plan for five years away and having no real idea of how we were going to get there. This was how the 3HAG was born.

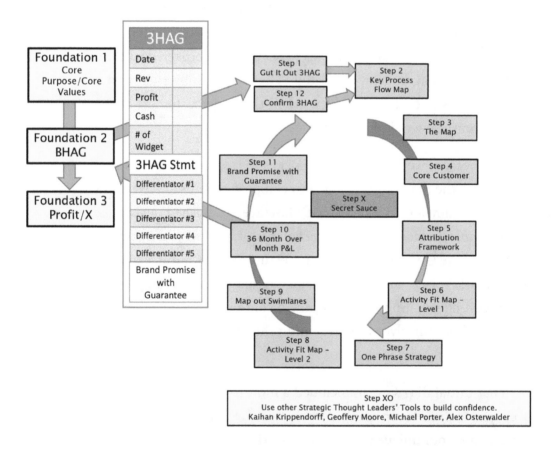

At the end of year four, we met strategic planning expert Verne Harnish, who shared with us his One-Page Strategic Plan tool. This was a practical way to capture our plan and keep it visible for the whole leadership team and company.

The Strategic Execution System that Ensures Your Strategy Is Not a Wild-Ass-Guess!

In order to create our One-Page Strategic Plan for Paradata, we were forced to ask and answer the following questions:

Column 1: Core Value: What are the company's core values?
Happy, Hungry, Humble.

Column 2: Core Purpose: Why does the company exist?
To create an organization that others value. And to create a great place to work.

BHAG: What is your company's 10-to-30-year goal?
The Leading Global Payment Processor.

(Note: These questions are derived from thought leaders Jim Collins and Patrick Lencioni, and we answered them in chapter 1.)

Column 3:

1. What is the year ending date of Year 3?

    a. June 30, 2004

2. What will the Fiscal Measures be:

    a. Cash in the bank: $2,000,000

    b. Revenue: $20,000,000

3. What are the "widgets" to get the company to this number:

    a. New merchants: 12,000

    b. Cumulative merchants: 30,000

4. What will the company be in 3 years? *(Write this statement with no numbers.)*

    a. The Leading North American Payment Provider

5. What are the 3–5 Key Capabilities we need in place to deliver on 1–4?

    a. Answer the phone service

    b. Set up merchants in less than an hour

Company Name: _____

Date: _____

Name: _____

Core Values	Core Purpose	3HAG (3 Years)	1HAG (1 Year)	90 Day Plan	Theme	Your Metrics

3HAG (3 Years): Future Date, Revenues, Profit, Cash

1HAG (1 Year): Yr Ending, Revenues, Expenses, Profit, Cash

90 Day Plan: Qtr Ending, Revenues, Expenses, Profit, Cash

| Core Competencies | CEO Actions | 3 Year Highly Achievable Goal | Annual Priorities | Quarterly Priorities | | Individual Quarterly Priorities |

| | Profit per X | 3–5 Differentiators | Non-Financial Critical # | Non-Financial Critical # | | |

| | 10+ Year Goal (Jim Collin's BHAG) | Brand Promise with Guarantee | | | | |

Adapted from Gazelles Inc.

Adapted from Gazelles Inc.

     c. Reseller Program

     d. Support any currency

  6. What do we want to be known for in 3 years?

     a. Making payments EASY!

Column 3 is where the 3HAG sprang to life. In the beginning, we gutted out these answers—and I recommend you do the same—but once we wrote it all down, we were not confident that these were the numbers and this was the position we wanted to be in. We needed to find a way to get more confident in these numbers and in where we were headed. The 3HAG framework was born through curiosity; we were seeking clarity and wanted to be confident that we were driving the company in the right direction.

Happily, you don't need to go through the process of developing your own framework the way we did at Paradata. The 3HAG framework is yours for the taking. Take a minute to fill in your 3HAG below. Right, wrong, or ugly, just write it down—*gut it out*. And ask the same questions of your leadership team.

Here is how to ask your leadership team to gut out your 3HAG:

a. Clarify what the ending date of your fiscal year is—3 years away. In the example for Paradata I shared, you can see that the date of our 3HAG was June 30, 2004. Clarify this with your team.

b. Ask, "How much cash do we want in the bank on this date, and what do we want our topline revenue to be for the fiscal year-end 3 years away?" Before any answers are verbalized, give each leader a 2 ×3 pad of sticky notes and ask them to write down their answer. When all leaders have written their answers down, have each leader share their answer and post it on a whiteboard or easel, grouping the answers that are similar. Once all leaders have presented their answers, look the answers over and discuss what the agreed-on "gutted-out" amount should be for Cash and Topline Revenue. At Paradata we agreed on these amounts:

- Cash in the bank: $2,000,000
- Revenue: $20,000,000

c. Next question: What will be the total widgets we will have to sell in order to achieve that cash in the bank and topline revenue? Before any answers are verbalized, ask leaders to write their answers on a pad of sticky notes and post.

d. Once all have presented their answers, look them over and discuss what the agreed-on gutted-out widget amount should be for Cash and Topline Revenue. Here are Paradata's figures:

- New merchants: 12,000
- Cumulative merchants: 30,000

e. Next ask, "What is our 3 Year Highly Achievable Goal for this organization? Write a sentence that describes our company in year three—written with no numbers." Before any answers are verbalized, ask leaders to write their answers on a pad of sticky notes and post them. Once all have presented their answers, look them over and discuss what the 3HAG—the 3 Year Highly Achievable Goal—of the organization should be. This might end up in draft form or you can ask a volunteer to take a picture of the sticky notes to write a 3HAG to present at the next meeting. But what you have is good enough for now. Paradata's 3HAG was to be the "Leading North American Payment Provider."

f. Next Question: "What are the 3–5 Key Capabilities we need in place to deliver on the goals stated above?" If there are eight or more people on the leadership team, break out into groups of two; otherwise, do this individually and come up with 3–5

Key Capabilities that must be in place by the end of year 3 to be able to achieve the fiscal and company goals. Before any answers are verbalized, ask each leader/group to write down their answer on a pad of sticky notes. When all leaders have written their answers down, have each leader/group share their answer and post it on a whiteboard or easel, grouping the answers that are similar. Once all have presented their answers, look over the answers and discuss what the 3–5 Key Capabilities/Differentiating Actions of the organization should be. This will end up in draft form for now, but it will be good enough. Paradata's four differentiating actions were as follows:

o **Answer the phone service**—When we were small and building this service, we answered the phone because we didn't have a phone system. We realized how important this was to our customers and resellers—it was a core need. If they were going to use a third-party payment service—like Paradata—they wanted someone to answer the phone because their topline revenue was at stake. As we grew, we eventually set up an enterprise phone system and made sure when the phone rang a team member answered. Part of this differentiation action was that we set up our operation in such a way that there would be no need to call us if we followed through on our operational goal of high availability of the platform. A big part of this capability was to make sure the phone did not ring—or at least, not often—and when it did, it was important to have a human being answer.

o **Set up merchants in less than an hour**—At the time we wrote this differentiating action, merchant account providers were projecting that they would be able to adjudicate a new merchant in less than an hour in 2–3 years. We needed to be ready for this. When this was gutted out, we could set up a new merchant in 60 days—which was more than 3 times faster than our competitors at the time. Then we brought it down to 30 days and to 7 days, and so on, over this time frame.

o **Reseller Program**—This was a differentiator due to the fact that no other service would allow a third party to co-brand or white label their service. This was core to our growth. We allowed large resellers to brand and resell our service. Now we were selling at high volume to a large reseller and sending only one bill rather than thousands. Royal Bank of Canada was our first white-label reseller. This was a big win.

o **Support any currency**—In order to be a global payment processor, we had to construct our platform to support any currency. And that we did.

g. Last step: With your leadership team, ask, "What do we want to be known for in 3 years?" Before any answers are verbalized, have each leader/group write down their answer. When all leaders/groups have done so, have each leader/group share their answer and post it on a whiteboard or easel, grouping the answers that are similar. Once all have presented their answers, look them over and discuss what the company wants to be known for in 3 years' time. This might end up in draft form, or you can ask a volunteer to take a picture of the sticky notes to discuss for the next meeting. But what you have is good enough for now. Paradata wanted to be known for making payments easy.

Now that you have your first gutted-out 3HAG, you are on your way. This is not perfect, but it is a great start for getting everyone driving toward the BHAG.

Over the next chapters, and over time with your team, you're going to revise and refine the gutted-out goals of your 3HAG. For now, don't worry about whether you got it right. The point is just to get it down on paper.

At Paradata we found the five-year goal was too far away to be highly achievable—or more importantly, to be predictable. We decided to shorten the time frame. Some people told us this was risky, because three years is so close that there was a higher probability of missing the goal. We thought exactly the opposite.

Because our goal was so close, we figured that we should be able to better align our achievement and thereby keep it from being a wild-ass-guess, which often happens with a five-year target. Three years is close enough that you can visualize it, discuss it, and debate it. The 3HAG doesn't let you get lazy by putting off activities that could otherwise catapult your company ahead of the competition.

Here is what our complete 3HAG strategy looked like for Paradata:

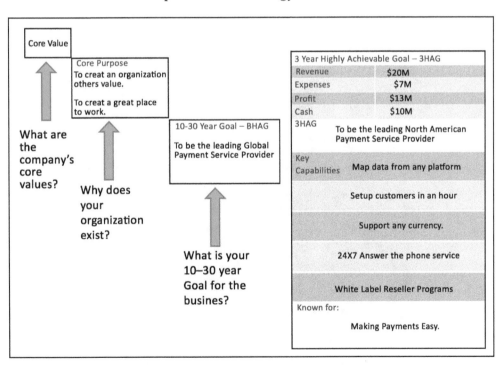

As you can see above, we described our Core Purpose—why Paradata existed in the first place—as well as our BHAG. Written out this way, you can see that your 3HAG is your road map to your BHAG. They must align.

When you have the right goals in place *and* you have a sturdy framework to guide you from one quarter to the next, you'll find that your confidence grows and your team's confidence grows. You develop a habit of checking on your goals and key metrics, meeting as a team to discuss what's next, and driving ahead toward the next goal. This iterative approach instills confidence that you and your team really are on your way to meeting your 3HAG. Confidence is a key part of the winning formula.

That's what happened at Paradata. Quarter over quarter, we continued to build confidence across the whole company. We did this by continuing to check in on goals and progress as a leadership team and keeping the rest of the team well informed. Our Strategic Pictures were displayed in our war room, and we reviewed them and updated them frequently as we moved forward.

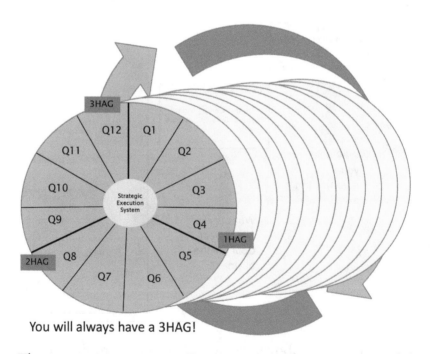

You will always have a 3HAG!

This is an iterative process. Executing your plan is a way to validate your plan. As you execute, you go back to your goals, your checklists, and your financials, and you assess your position. You adjust. You refine. You get better with each lap. You get more confident. Maybe you miss your goals in the first and second quarters, but you're close by quarter three. Pretty soon the first year is under your belt, and you're accelerating into quarters four, five, and six—and eventually, toward your 3HAG.

For each quarter at Paradata, we determined the actions the team needed to take in order to get us where we needed to be. Our team gathered every week, month, and quarter to stay focused on our 3HAG and Annual Plan. We analyzed our external environment and the internal environment the company was playing in—which is crucial—and we made changes accordingly, to ensure that we were moving the company continuously to a unique and valuable position. And with that clarity, our confidence and momentum continued to grow.

BHAG + 3HAG = Your Compass

Your BHAG is your true north. By setting that 10-to-30-year goal, you're working with everyone on your team, guiding where the company is going to end up. It's your North Star.

Your 3HAG makes your BHAG believable. Your 3HAG is the stepping-stone to the end goal. It's the route you'll take to get there and the map that shows every twist and turn along the way. There are fewer surprises waiting for you when you've already charted your course in your 3HAG. That's not to say you won't encounter obstacles—far from it. But if you've planned for the unexpected, your 3HAG will help you navigate every obstacle that appears.

Paradata was no quick success, that's for sure. That is mainly because we got off to a rocky, unclear start—not because we didn't have money in the bank—we did—and lots. We got off to a rocky start because we were not clear on how we were going to *make* money in

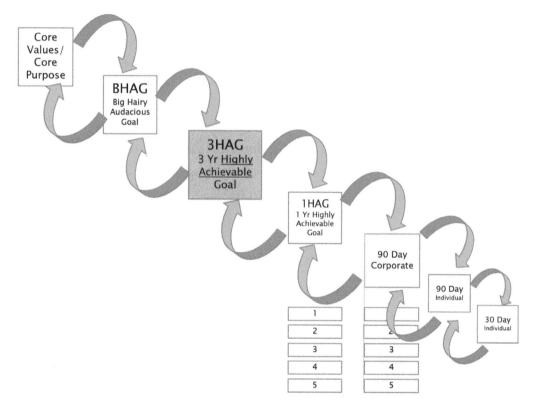

the first quarter and every quarter. Making money is key. But once we developed the 3HAG framework, growing the company became a whole lot easier, and so did making money. And as I mentioned in chapter 1, by the time I got to my second company, Subserveo, we were able to turn it into a success and sell it in just over three years, thanks to our 3HAG. Since becoming a coach, I've found myself describing the 3HAG as the goose that lays the golden eggs. If you follow this framework, and if you make it into a repeatable, habitual system in your company, then your company will be a goose that lays golden eggs every time!

Check-in

1. Gut out your first 3HAG ✓

2. Create your Key Process Flow Map

3. Create your Market Map

CHAPTER TAKEAWAYS

✔ *Strategy* is how a company creates a unique and valuable position through a set of differentiating actions.

✔ Create your first gutted-out 3HAG!

✔ Your 3HAG will build confidence in your strategy, your company, and your team. It's your road map to reach your ultimate goal—your BHAG.

Chapter 4

Map It:
Internal and External

Knowing yourself is the beginning of all wisdom.
—Aristotle

In the last chapter, you completed your first gutted-out 3HAG. Now we need to build on this gutted-out 3HAG, adding to our confidence by visualizing the story through key Strategic Pictures. These pictures keep your strategy in front of you and the team, as well as make it easier to review, confirm, and evolve. This refinement comes from a continuous analysis both externally and internally. We will map out the market you are playing in by using the Market Map, and we will also map out the key functional processes in your business that are crucial to making money, through the Key Process Flow Map (KPFM).

Each of the components of the 3HAG will end up on your wall. They will be in the form of sticky notes, drawn maps, and process flows—all in the name of confidence. This is what I call a Strategic Picture. It is nothing fancy—just a reminder of the thinking process that got us to this point, what we are confident about, and what we need to confirm or reconfirm. Such simple pictures tell a powerful strategic story of your company.

The Key Process Flow Map

Now that we have gutted out our 3HAG, let's take the next step—to map out the three to six key functional processes in your company that make the company money. These are *internal*, functional activities like marketing, sales, manufacturing, and finance. We don't only want to map them out—we also want to identify which leader is functionally accountable for these key processes.

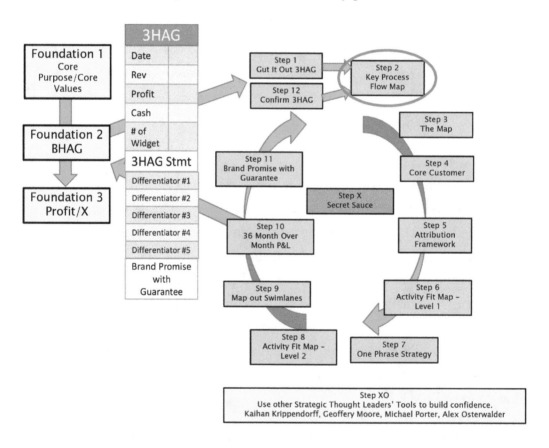

Your Key Process Flow Map (KPFM) allows you and your team to do an internal analysis of your company. The most effective way to execute on the strategy in your 3HAG is to conduct an ongoing analysis of the external environment—which we will do next in our Market Map—as well as your internal environment, which you're now going to capture in your KPFM.

The KPFM identifies which functions are key at your company to making money, how you can improve on them to make your business run more efficiently, who is accountable, and where some strategic advantage may be realized. It will also show where you are aligned with your 3HAG. What's more, through the process of creating your KPFM, you may even identify your "secret sauce," which will give you an up to *tenfold* advantage in the marketplace.

Below is a KPFM for Paradata.

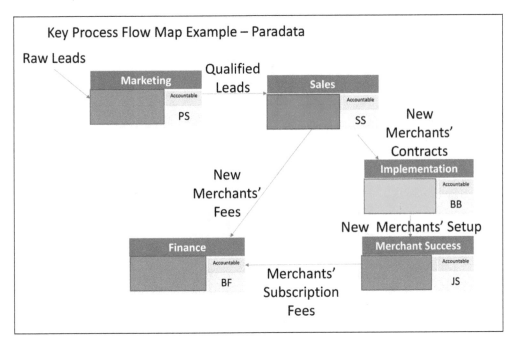

At Paradata, the key functions that we highlighted included a marketing function, a sales function, an implementation function, a finance function, and a merchant success function.

Whether I am working with very mature or very young companies, the result of mapping how a company makes money provides the same clarity. I am always amazed that such a simple map can have such an impact to focus the leadership team on how the company makes money. To create your company's KPFM, do the following with your leadership team:

Organizational Function Chart

1. Have each leader fill out the NAME column in the Organizational Function Chart adapted from Gazelles Growth Tools. This chart can be found at http://www.shannonsusko.com/.

Organizational Function Chart

Scorecard	Functional Role	NAME	90 Day One Page Plan	Leading Critical #	Lagging Metric
	Head of Company				
	Marketing				
	Sales				
	Operations				
	Manufacturing/ Development				
	Finance				
	Treasury				
	Controller				
	HR/Learning/ People				
	Information Technology				
	Customer Success				

Adapted from Verne Harnish's Function Accountability Chart

2. Once this is filled out, re-create this chart on the whiteboard or easel pad and have each leader call out who they had in each function, one by one; write down all the names shared for each function. And if there are any changes to the functional names—since those on the chart are generic—please make those agreed-upon adjustments as well.

Function	Name
Head of Company	Shannon
Marketing	Peter
Sales	Shannon
Implementation	Ben
Development	Zac
Finance	Beth
Treasury	Beth
Controller	Beth
IT/IS	Bojan
People/Learning	Betsy
Merchant Success	Jeff

3. Once you have input from all the leaders, go back to the top and start with "Head of Company" and agree on who is accountable for that function. Do the same for marketing, sales, and the other functions. We are trying to identify where you are clear that one person owns the function, which functions have no names (and who should be listed), and functions that clearly have more than one person contributing, but no clear owner.

4. This is a Strategic Picture. I recommend you put it up on the wall and leave it. Revisit it every quarterly meeting, at a minimum. This chart helps provide the clarity required in order to have absolute accountability for the key functions of the company.

5. This Organization Function Chart should also map directly to your organizational chart. This chart should be founded upon the functions of your company, and then add the names of team members accountable for these functional positions.

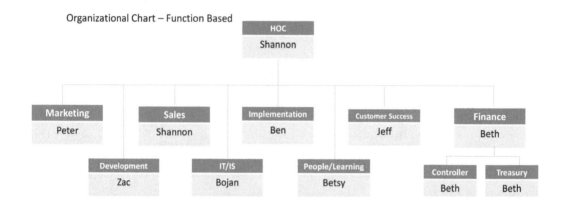

Organizational Chart – Function Based

The organizational chart shown above identifies the key functional positions in the company; it shows who is accountable and, at this point in time, the Head of Company (HOC or CEO) is wearing two hats—so to speak—CEO and Sales. The Organizational Function Chart and the organizational chart mapped out should reveal the following: whether one person or many people are accountable for too many roles, and/or that no one is accountable for a key function in your company, either because no one is doing this role or too many people are contributing to the role with no one ultimately owning it.

Now that you have clarified your organizational functions, you and your team can clearly map out the KPFM:

1. Break the leadership team into groups of two to three.

2. Ask each group to come up with the three to six key functional processes that make the company money. Get the groups to write each one down on a separate sticky note. The functions being written down should be a function highlighted in the Organizational Function Chart.

3. Next, ask the group to draw/map how those functions interact *within* your company, as was done above in the KPFM example for Paradata.

4. Identify the inputs to each function and the outputs.

5. After all the groups have mapped out the Key Process flow, get each group to present their flows. You will be surprised at all the variations. Come to an agreement on one flow that reflects your team KPFM.

6. Ask the leadership team who owns each function. This has already been done in creating the Organizational Function Chart, but it's a great idea to ask again—as now they are stepping up and telling the team they are accountable.

7. Color-code these functions: green for all systems go, yellow for potential issues, and red for trouble that must be fixed ASAP. Do this color-coding every quarter by asking the functional owner to color-code their function. In a high-growth company, it's hard to keep all functions green at one time. If one area becomes super green, another area could become imbalanced with red as it was not ready for the increased numbers. You get the picture.

8. For each key function, identify how long it takes to go from a lead to actually putting money in the bank by listing the number of days for each functional process and adding up all the days for each function listed in your KPFM.

9. Put the KPFM on the wall and keep it updated and alive. The KPFM is a view for all team members as to where they are accountable to contribute to the company making money. This is another Strategic Picture that should be available for continuous review.

Looking at Paradata's KPFM, we can see that raw leads flow into Marketing, and qualified leads flow out of Marketing to Sales. Sales then takes each qualified lead, converts the opportunity, and sells a payment-processing service to a new merchant. That new merchant then flows to Implementation, and dollars flow to Finance by way of a contract. The newly sold merchant becomes a live merchant and flows to Customer Success, whose goal is to keep merchants happy and spending the money that the Finance team collects.

In our map, all these processes function well except for Sales, which is red, and Implementation, which is yellow. Sales was red at the time of this KPFM due to the fact that we were implementing an immediate improvement to our sales process that would speed up the sales process by ten days. And Implementation was yellow because the team had not yet instituted certain processes that would shorten the amount of time to implement a new merchant. If one of your company's processes has urgent issues that need to be solved, color that function red. If there are things that need to be fixed but are not urgent, color it yellow. If a function is running smoothly right now, color it green.

A team leader who is responsible for, or "owns," each of these key business functions is clearly accountable for how the process is operating. When your leadership team is together, everyone can see how their particular function operates in relation to the other functions. If there's a problem, your strategy meeting is the ideal time to discuss solutions.

Keep the KPFM on the meeting room wall permanently, so that all your team leaders can analyze and discuss changes at each meeting when applicable. Regular use of the KPFM helps with overall strategic evaluation, operations flow, and accountability. It also builds team confidence—and puts cash in the bank sooner.

I have observed that most companies do a great job on external analysis but are likely to take their internal processes for granted: "We already know what we're doing. We've been serving these customers for twenty years. Why do we need to analyze these processes now?"

The answer lies in the simple truth that both internal and external forces are continually changing. It doesn't matter whether you're a large or small company; the forces within and beyond your business are never static. The KPFM shows how your internal processes interact in order to keep your team focused on strategic goals. It's a Strategic Picture that clarifies exactly how you're going to make money in an ever-changing environment.

The Market Map

The secret to successful strategy execution is deciding to put your company in the white space that is open in your market. The white space is where your company is in its own dimension, competing to be unique rather than to be the best. You can't just assume or hope that your company will move into a white space.

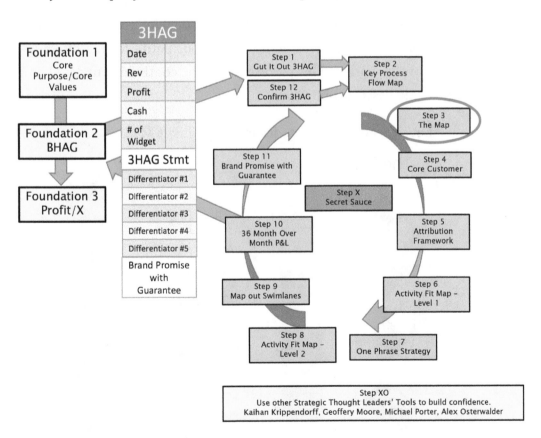

Getting your company there requires effort and a smart strategy that evolves, as necessary, with the market. We're going to start by using a tool called the "Market Map" so that you can see who loves you, who hates you, who your biggest competitors are, and who holds the most power and leverage in the overall marketplace. All of this is important information.

When we started at Paradata, we were groping in the dark for a valuable market position. My team and I had pivoted into an industry in which none of us were experts, so we desperately needed to draw out who all the players were and how information flowed from one end of the marketplace to the other. Even if you consider yourself an expert in your industry, this tool—and the Strategic Picture you'll create—is extremely helpful because it enables you to see all this information in one place. It also gives your entire team a bird's-eye view of the market. This picture should be continually updated on a quarterly basis at minimum.

Let's go step-by-step to fill in your Market Map.

The Map

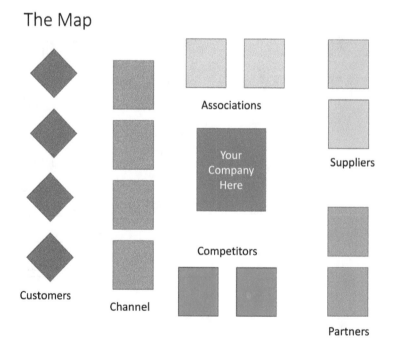

We'll fill in the Market Map from left to right. We'll draw how you go to market (how you're making money) on the left side, while the right side will show your supply chain (where you're spending money).

- **Step One:** Get a massive sheet of blank paper and a pad of sticky notes. In the middle of the sheet, draw a box and write your company's name in it.

- **Step Two:** Go to the left side of the paper and, from top to bottom, draw or use sticky notes to map all the customers—or "buyers"—in your industry. (You may not be in business with these buyers yet, but if they exist in your marketplace, you need to map them in.) In the case of Paradata, the buyers were different-size merchants in the United States and Canada. For Paradata's Market Map, we drew out all these potential buyers in the industry as diamonds (you should use different shapes to differentiate between different groups). Some businesses were more relevant to us than others, which is why we drew multiple diamonds around the medium-size businesses in Canada and the United States.

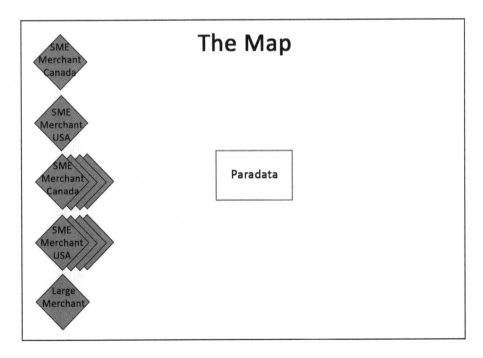

- **Step Three:** Draw possible resellers, referrals, or secondary channels through which you might reach your customers. *Channels* are conduits that may (or may not) allow you to reach your customers. Even though there may be channels in your marketplace that you don't plan on using, think of channels as players on the field. You've got to map them, regardless of whether you're in direct contact with them.

- **Step Four:** Draw the connections (if any) between your company, your channels, and your customers.

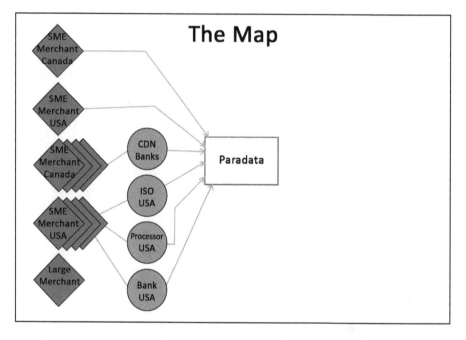

Now you've mapped out your relationships for the left side of the page.

In Paradata's case, our goal was not to sell directly to businesses. We ultimately wanted to work exclusively with third-party channels, like American banks and processors, to reach our medium-size customers. However, as we mapped this out, we learned that, rather than using third-party channels, we had gone directly to small- and medium-size merchants when Paradata was just getting started.

That was an important insight, and it helped direct where we would go next. We focused ourselves on the goal of getting one to five of the biggest banks in Canada, in other words, on acquiring ten to twenty of Royal Bank of Canada's customers. In fact, Royal Bank ended up helping us out in a big way. They referred *all* their clients to us because they didn't have a way to process their customers' payments through the internet, and we did. That happened thanks to our Market Map.

In other words, the important aspect of this part of the Market Map was to see that Paradata sold directly to small- and medium-size Canadian merchants. We went into the American marketplace and approached the top resellers and their customers, and we started building a portfolio. But in the beginning, we had some direct merchants that we billed monthly. We charged some of these clients via credit card, and others paid us an annual payment.

Ultimately, we wanted to work through channels—resellers, in essence—because secondary channels presented the best way to position Paradata as different from other credit processors in the marketplace. We didn't mind another organization branding our platform (white labeling) and selling it through their network, so that was what we focused on. When we met with these resellers, it was an easy sell, because we had already proven ourselves with our direct-sales customers.

We chose to focus on resellers because that was the easiest and quickest way to scale the business. Now we could send one invoice to Royal Bank of Canada, which would turn around and invoice hundreds of merchants to whom they had sold our solution. Instead of us invoicing those hundreds of merchants ourselves, we had Royal Bank doing the heavy lifting for us.

It's worth noting here that we never went after large merchants, because we knew that they had their own in-house payment-processing services, but we included them on the Market Map because they were in our market. If you're a leader who believes you *should* go after large merchants but haven't yet done it, the Market Map makes this clear and facilitates the conversation about making that next step. And over time you can see who and what is evolving in the marketplace.

- **Step Five:** Go to the far right of the paper and write down all the companies that supply this market—these are the places where your company spends money. Also write down the names of other suppliers with whom you may not do business but who operate in the market.

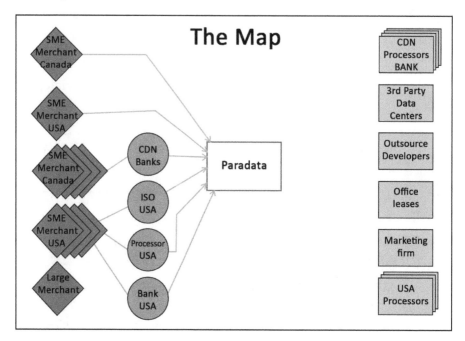

Now we had a clear view of where Paradata was spending money. We were paying our outsourced software developers, marketing firms, and office leases. Your expenses will vary. Be sure to include every place your company spends money.

You may wonder why writing this down is important. After all, if you've got a CFO, you already know where you send checks every month. But drawing a map of where you spend your money gives everyone on your team a view of this aspect of the business.

These suppliers may not even target your market specifically—software developers, for instance, service pretty much every industry—but it's important to include them, because your company is going to spend dollars on the back end of this supply chain to facilitate bringing your product or service to market.

Since Paradata was a payment-processing company, we didn't have an inventory. But if you run a manufacturing company, the right side of your Market Map will be filled with inventory as well.

- **Step Six:** Draw lines to indicate your relationships with your suppliers. There may be suppliers in your marketplace with whom you don't yet have relationships.

- **Step Seven:** Draw in all your competitors. There may be competitors in the marketplace who don't concern you, but you need to include them anyway because they exist. You and your team need to be aware of them. Their presence may change how your company does business someday.

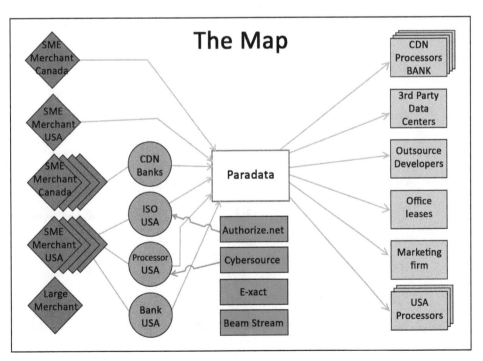

Paradata's Market Map showed four competitors: Authorize.net, Cybersource, E-xact, and Beanstream. Of those, our biggest competitors were Authorize.net and Cybersource, two American payment-processing companies. We didn't focus too much on E-xact and Beanstream, our Canadian competitors, but we included them nevertheless.

- **Step Eight:** Draw your competitors' relationships to the channels and buyers in the marketplace. You want to see if your competitors' relationships are similar to yours. What you're looking for is as little overlap as possible, which would mean you're not in direct competition with your competitors and that you've staked out your own white space.

  Those relationships have been drawn in the map below. You'll see that Authorize.net and Cybersource had relationships with American channels and independent sales organizations—the same as Paradata—but they did not have relationships with the Canadian or American banks, which made them different from Paradata.

  Our Canadian competitors at the time could only process Canadian transactions, whereas Paradata had built a global platform that could process *any* currency. I didn't draw the relationships between E-xact and Beanstream because they were going direct to Canadian customers and didn't work through any channels at the time. (Note: Market Maps get full awfully quickly! If this happens to you, it's okay to draw a global Market Map and then additional Market Maps per region.)

  The Market Map also showed that there was some overlap between Paradata and our competitors. Less overlap, of course, is always better.

- **Step Nine:** At the very top of the page, add all the businesses or associations (trade organizations, business groups, chambers of commerce) relevant to your company. Then draw arrows to those entities with which you have working relationships.

Key:

ETA: Electronic Transaction Association

WNET: Women Networking in Transactions

NSBA: National Small Business Association

WCC: Whistler Chamber of Commerce

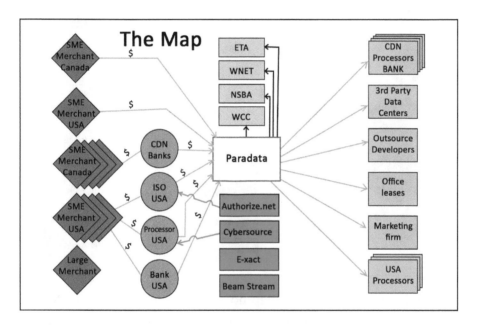

Paradata had working partnerships with lots of different trade associations—in fact, as you can see from our Market Map, we had working relationships with every relevant association within our marketplace. And although we were members of the Whistler Chamber of Commerce, we had a transactional relationship with them, too: the WCC included many small businesses for which we processed direct merchant accounts. Remember, working small was part of our initial strategy. We wanted to work directly with merchants until we grew big enough that Royal Bank would approach us and say, "Hey, Paradata, we'd like to brand your payment-processing solutions and sell them to our customers."

- **Step Ten:** Follow the dollar. Draw where dollars are flowing to and from your business. Make sure that you're drawing money going in both directions to distinguish from relationships where money isn't flowing. Then, rather than give a dollar amount for each relationship, estimate the percentage of overall dollars coming and going in each channel.

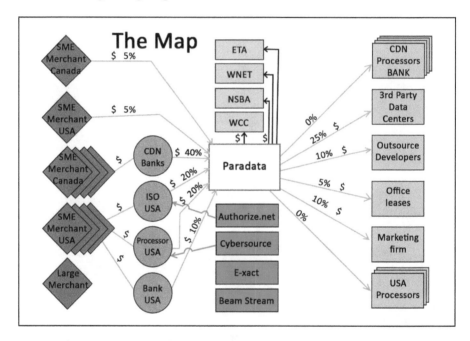

Looking at our Market Map now, we can see that 40 percent of our revenue was coming from Canadian banks at the time we drew this. Fifty percent of our revenue was coming from the United States through our channels. Two of those channels represented 20 percent of our revenue coming from processors. Overall, the map shows that we were generating half of our revenue from the United States, and the other half from Canada. Over time, these percentages changed to roughly 65/35 (US/Canadian) and our Market Map evolved accordingly. This section is important because it gives an immediate overview of where money is flowing, who's getting most of it, and why.

Once we drew out all our relationships, we could easily see who had the power on the playing field. At this point, we were not exchanging any money with the Canadian and US processors, and we did not have any contractual relationship whatsoever. This was a high-risk situation. We made money by processing merchant transactions, but the processors could have turned us off at any time. To address this, we carefully built a merchant base, one processor at a time. This helped to build our credibility with our now mutual customers and decreased the power these processors had in the marketplace, so they would never turn us off.

Then we went to each processor/bank and developed a reseller or referral relationship with that processor—once again, to decrease our risk and increase our power. Paradata's ultimate goal was to get into the back office of the merchants and in between the bank and its merchants. Eventually we were able to put contractual relationships in place with the processors—very key! In the meantime, the Market Map showed everyone in our company that we were working on both front- and back-end relationships with the same company.

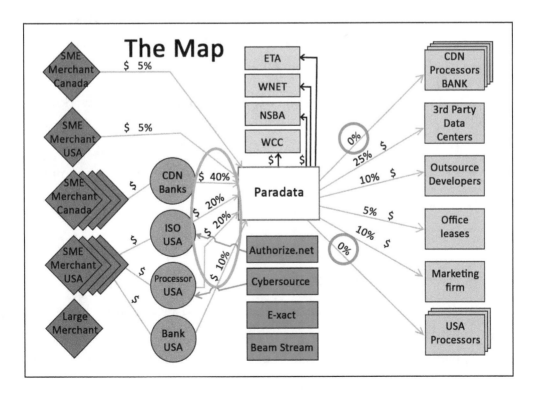

Those areas you see circled in red were red flags for us. They demonstrated areas where Paradata was not in a powerful position and where we wanted to focus on changing that dynamic. Over time, as those relationships changed, those red circles changed to green. The green circles highlighted our positions of power.

As you can see, the Market Map gets messy as you add more and more detail. If you run a multinational company, consider creating separate maps for each country where you do business. Paradata ultimately created a map for each country. Separate maps for separate countries also allow you to differentiate among various country requirements.

What the Market Map Reveals about Your Company

Drawing out the marketplace—your playing field—in the Market Map allows you to see all the players on the field. The goal of the Market Map is to get a good view of all these players, where your company fits in, and what actions you might need to take as a result of a poor position. This also gives your whole team a visual understanding of where you stand and which areas need work.

When I work one-on-one with clients or host in-house workshops, many people at this step are surprised by the difference between what they thought their position was in the market and what it really is. Getting clear about this map is essential as you grow your company.

Now you have your Market Map! Make sure that you keep it up to date and visible to all.

Growing Confidence

The last couple of chapters have covered a lot of ground, and your head may be spinning. But as you do this essential work to analyze your market, you'll feel the benefit of a growing confidence. You now have a handle on where your business fits in its larger ecosystem. You're well on your way to establishing your unique and valuable position in your marketplace—and driving toward your 3HAG.

In the next chapter we'll discover your Core Customer—and how that builds the confidence you and your team will need to continue pursuing your 3HAG.

Check-in

1. Gut out your first 3HAG ✓

2. Create your Key Process Flow Map ✓

3. Create your Market Map ✓

4. Define your Core Customer

CHAPTER TAKEAWAYS

✔ *White space* is the space in the marketplace where your organization is unique and valuable to your targeted Core Customer.

✔ *The Key Process Flow Map (KPFM)* is an internal analysis that shows the three to six functions that drive your business and are critical to bringing in cash. (Note: This tool is a Strategic Picture.)

✔ *The Market Map* is a tool to be used on a continuous basis to help everyone on your team see the bird's-eye view of the marketplace. (Note: This tool is a Strategic Picture.)

Chapter 5

Core Customer: Who Is Your Who?

The easiest and most profitable growth will be achieved by adding additional customers very much like your current most valuable customer.
—Robert Bloom

M any high-growth companies spend 98 percent of their business day executing—in other words, putting out fires and handling day-to-day operations. But productive strategy planning will require more than just 2 percent of your time.

Back when we were just getting Paradata off the ground, we used to joke that all our strategy meetings were done in the middle of the night, because we were too busy operating our business the rest of the time. The truth is that the more time you spend on strategy with your team (not by yourself!), the better the whole team will execute, because the clearer everyone will be on the day-to-day decisions that drive your 3HAG and BHAG.

Let's go back to Michael Porter's definition of strategy: creating a unique and valuable position involving a set of differentiating actions. Developing a strategy is all about making decisions. You must decide what you are going to do and what you are *not* going to do, all in the context of your Core Customer.

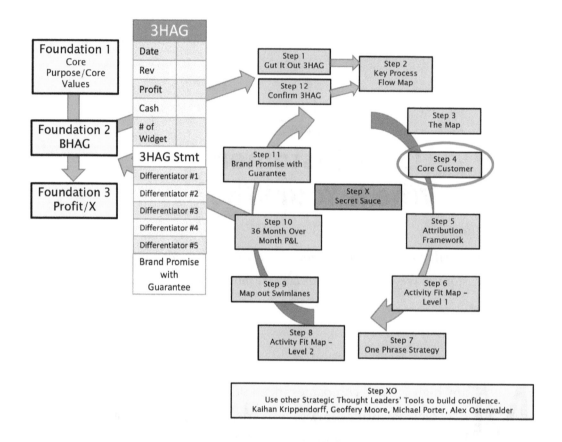

Identify and Understand Your Core Customer

"We have 35,000 customers, and you want me to describe our *Core Customer?*"

Yes. Here's why.

Knowing your Core Customer, right down to the individual, is not about marketing, per se. It's about strategy. Knowing the biggest needs of this individual will help you carve out a unique and valuable position by revealing what differentiating actions are meaningful to your Core Customers.

If your company has 35,000 customers, it's quite possible that 60 percent of them are your Core Customers who are generating your profit, and the rest actually cost you more money than they're worth.

It may look like you're making some topline revenue from those non–Core Customers, but their overall lack of profitability could be killing your organization. When you focus on the customers who provide the greatest return, and you direct all your resources toward those Core Customers, you'll be rewarded in growth and profitability.

Knowing your Core Customer is always beneficial, whether you run a start-up or lead a well-established legacy company. Core Customer identification may even be more important for mature companies if they haven't examined their customer base for a couple of decades.

So who is *your* Core Customer?

We're going to identify your Core Customer using a process developed by Robert Bloom, a business development analyst known throughout the coaching community for helping Nestlé, Southwest Airlines, and Zales—as well as various nonprofits and start-ups—find their Core Customers. Bloom's innovative 2007 book, *The Inside Advantage: The Strategy that Unlocks the Hidden Growth in Your Business*, details how team leaders can identify what their company does well and tells them how to find their most valuable customers.[1]

In this book, we'll be working from his definition of *Core Customer*, because it's one of the clearest definitions out there. Bloom defines a Core Customer as *an individual person*—not a population segment or a market segment or a company—who will buy from your company for *optimal profit*. Simple. This means you've got to get down to eye level to understand the person who will ultimately decide to buy from you.

Who Is Your *Who*?

Below is the worksheet for identifying your Core Customer. Think of this worksheet as peeling back the layers of an onion—each layer

---

1 Robert H. Bloom, *The Inside Advantage: The Strategy that Unlocks the Hidden Growth in Your Business* (New York: McGraw-Hill, 2008).

Detailed Core Customer Analysis

Core Customer Description: (Describe the person in detail who will make the decision to buy at a profit. 50 words or less)			
Core Need: (the primary reason the core customer wil buy your product or service)			
Drivers: (Key benefits offered to satisfy the core customer need)			

revealing what matters most to your Core Customer and therefore how you should focus your resources to provide what that customer wants.

Note: There are more worksheets at http://www.shannonsusko.com. I use many different analyses when working with companies to ensure that we are focused on the Core Customer. I like to start with this one as it provides easy-to-answer questions, and if you think you have more than one Core Customer, the columns allow you to compare. This is a good tool for the first analysis.

At Paradata, our Core Customer was a man between forty and sixty-five years old, most likely married with kids, who coached Little League and carried a mobile phone. He was stretched for time and loved to sell. We named him Peter. He was part of our reseller channel because the reseller channel was how we went to market.

If you looked more superficially at our business model, it would have appeared that our Core Customer was the end merchant who

Core Customer Example – Paradata

processed payments. But it was actually Peter, who was a sales leader at our reseller and who needed to add services like ours to sell more credit-card merchant accounts. What mattered most to him was making money and selling more: he wanted to sell to the merchant, he wanted the sale to be easy, and he wanted the product to simply *work* so he didn't have to take any support calls.

We went so far as to create a cardboard cutout of Peter, and then we brought him to all of our meetings to help us stay focused on our Who. This may seem absurd, but the endgame requires knowing your Core Customer. (Bringing a cardboard cutout of a customer isn't original to my team, by the way; Amazon CEO Jeff Bezos is widely known for leaving a chair empty at team meetings to represent his Core Customer. If you need proof that knowing your Core Customer will bring in the cash, look no further than that.)

For Companies Without Customers

Some companies don't have customers . . . yet. Maybe they're pivoting to a new space, or debuting a new product, or the business is brand-new. Defining your Core Customer, right down to the person, is foundational to your strategy. Do *not* skip this step, even if you haven't yet had your first customer. Define your *Who.*

Remember, confidence comes from building a solid, clear strategy. You're unlikely to do that without knowing your Core Customer. Defining your Core Customer shows you where you fit in the marketplace—and whether there are enough Core Customers to make money. I'll say it again: Don't skip this step! It's what your strategy is founded upon. I only wish we had done this when we first started Paradata.

For Mature Companies

It's crucial for mature companies to define their Core Customers. In many cases mature companies have not looked closely at their Core Customers for years, and due to shifting market forces, things have changed. Are there enough Core Customers in your market to support your enterprise?

This tool also will help you see whether you've cornered the Core Customer in your marketplace, or whether you need to evolve your strategy to become more focused on being valuable to your most profitable customers rather than anyone who gives your company a look. This analysis shows you where to direct the majority of your resources: toward those Core Customers who are the easiest to serve and from whom you will profit most.

Here are some key questions to review with the leadership team to evaluate your current customers to determine who among them is your Core Customer:

Six Steps to Your Core Customer Based on Robert Bloom's *Inside Advantage*	
GOAL: A statement that clearly illustrates your Core Customer.	
1	Add to the list above competitor's customers that you currently want as well.
2	Put an asterisk next to customers who are perceived as most valuable.
3	Discuss with your team what other valuable clients to add to the list.
4	Who are your highest priority customers? Underline the customers that you want to keep.
5	Look at <u>just</u> these high priority customers: a. Define these individuals using two or three specific words or phrases. b. What are their specific, individual traits or characteristics? c. Why are they high priority for you? d. What makes them a good fit for your company's culture or specific product/service offering? e. Does the team like working with these customers? Why? f. At this point, just list as much information about the customer as you can, then pull it together in a definition that's about 20 words long. Your definition won't be perfect.
6	Come up with a list of 10–15 things that the Core Customer you've identified desires.
7	Additional Step for Clarity: Collect some insights from those on your team who interact with customers most often and even from the customers themselves about what they want.
8	High Priority Customers—profitable? Review through an analysis to make sure your high priority customers are profitable.

In certain cases, this work will lead to some uncomfortable discussions, as there may be certain truths that your team would rather not face. Perhaps there are fewer of your Core Customers now than there were ten years ago. Perhaps your product or service is no longer so relevant. Or perhaps the continual change of the marketplace now requires you to make some important tweaks. Whatever you discover in this exercise is valuable information that will help you evolve your strategy. (Note: http://www.shannonsusko.com/ has many tools to define and analyze your Core Customer.)

Check-in

1. Gut out your first 3HAG ✓
2. Create your Key Process Flow Map ✓
3. Create your Market Map ✓
4. Define your Core Customer ✓
5. Create your Attribution Framework
6. Name your 3–5 Differentiating Actions by completing your Activity Fit Map
7. Draw your Activity Fit Map II
8. Summarize your One-Phrase Strategy

You've already tackled the first four items on this list. Now you're ready to move on to creating your Attribution Framework. From there we'll have enough information to define your company's 3–5 Differentiating Actions. After that, we'll check for fit. That's where you decide whether the key activities your company performs actually differentiate you from your competitors.

So let's turn to the Attribution Framework.

CHAPTER TAKEAWAYS

✔ *A Core Customer* is *an individual person* who will buy what he or she needs from your company in a way that generates *optimal profit*.

Chapter 6

3–5 Differentiating Actions to Create Your Unique and Valuable Position

If there were only one ideal position, there would be no need for strategy.
—Michael Porter

Michael Porter's work made strategy clear. It made sense that as a company we should not be competing head-to-head with another company on single features; rather, we needed to find a Core Customer, as described in the last chapter, that our company could serve on its own dimension, one that no one else could serve due to our interdependent 3–5 Differentiating Actions. Understanding this really made it clear to the Paradata and Subserveo teams that even though we were offering a service that other providers were also offering, we should serve a Core Customer who had particular needs that only we could serve at a profit.

Find Your Dimension

Differentiating your company from the competition is important, but it's especially important if your company is competing in a *commoditized marketplace*, in which every other business is positioned essentially in the same dimension. A commoditized marketplace is

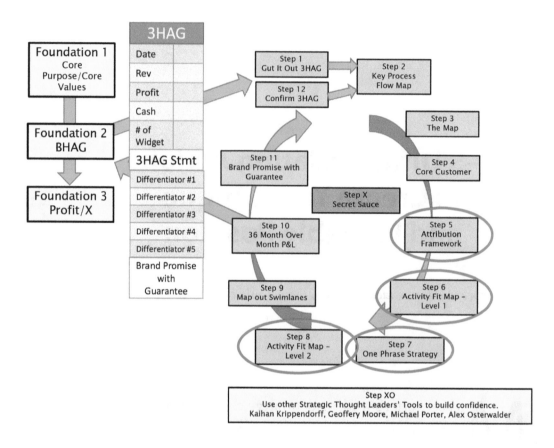

usually a race to the bottom, with everyone competing on price. In a sense, this is what's happening right now in retail. Everyone from Macy's to the Gap is competing on price, which means they're all leveraging similar inventory but trying to outdo one another with lower prices.[1] And it's not working; many retail outlets are closing stores. In contrast, TJ Maxx is one company that's winning in the retail sphere, because even though its core differentiating actions revolve around low prices, the entire business is structured to offer low prices on regularly revolving product.

In a commoditized marketplace you lack the power to set your prices, because your competitors can always undercut you. Everyone

---

1 Laura Heller, "Retailers in a Race to the Bottom (and How to Stop It), Retail, *Forbes.com*, May 24, 2016, https://www.forbes.com/sites/lauraheller/2016/05/24/retailers-in-a-race-to-the-bottom-and-how-to-stop-it/ - 610445ba85dd.

is competing on the same actions—in other words, no one is differentiating. Or rather, they are only differentiating on one thing: price.

In contrast, a unique and valuable position is based on at least 3–5 interdependent Differentiating Actions. If a competitor copied any single one of these actions, it would not upend your unique and valuable position.

Consider Southwest Airlines, which chose to distinguish itself from its competitors with not one or two but *six* differentiating actions. The company created a unique and valuable position in the marketplace by becoming *the* low-cost, no-frills airline, and they did it from soup to nuts, throughout the whole organization. They aligned the whole enterprise behind their strategy.

Southwest is the largest low-cost, domestic airline carrier in the United States. The company's *unique and valuable position* is to deliver low-cost service on point-to-point routes through secondary airports, a strategy that they chose because they believed it mattered to their Core Customer. These were the company's six key differentiating actions:

1. Automated ticketing
2. Frequent departures
3. Low ticket prices
4. Short-haul, point-to-point routes between secondary airports and midsize cities
5. Limited passenger service
6. High aircraft utilization

Southwest's strategy also included modernizing its fleet, incorporating high-density seating arrangements, no seat assignments, and no food service. All these actions kept costs low but demand high. They provided exactly what their Core Customer needed. Southwest became wildly successful.

Trying to Compete on Price Alone:
The Tale of Continental Lite

Continental Airlines is a traditional, full-service, full-fare "legacy" airline. At the same time, however, it tried to compete with Southwest on point-to-point routes by introducing a spin-off service called Continental Lite. Continental Lite eliminated in-flight meals and first-class seating, and lowered fares and turnaround times.

But the airline was unwilling to make *strategic trade-offs*, so it continued to provide full-service amenities on long-haul flights. It also continued to pay travel agent commissions and flubbed baggage transfers between connecting flights, which led to delayed departures and arrivals, thereby reneging on its promise of quick turnaround. This, naturally, led to many unhappy customers.

Meanwhile, Continental Lite continued to slash prices, which meant the airline was generating less revenue to pay for its full-service amenities. As a result, Continental had to slash frequent-flyer benefits and reduce commissions to travel agents. The airline suffered a colossal failure: millions of dollars in lost revenue, the firing of its CEO, and the end of Continental Lite.[2]

In effect, Continental had tried to copy Southwest's strategy. But rather than embrace the entire strategy—including automated ticketing, no baggage transfers, no long-haul flights, and so on—they simply tried to compete on price. That is, they tried to compete on *only one* of Southwest's differentiating actions. And this left Continental's other operations vulnerable and compromised. They did not align the whole company behind their strategy.

---

2 Adam Bryant, "Continental Is Dropping 'Lite' Service," Company Reports, *New York Times*, April 14, 1995, http://www.nytimes.com/1995/04/14/business/company-reports-continental-is-dropping-lite-service.html.

The lesson here is that your strategy must include a combination of differentiating actions with interlocking components that reinforce your company's entire ethos. Mapping this out, seeing it, and understanding it will give you the clarity and confidence to *execute it* (not to mention to refine it and update it as necessary).

On the whole, the airline industry is not profitable, but Southwest has made itself one of the most profitable airlines in the world, enjoying an industry record of more than forty consecutive years of profitability.[3] Southwest was never coy about what the company was doing—disrupting the airline status quo. Its strategy has been dissected endlessly, but no one has been able to copy it successfully in North America.

Find Your Most Profitable Dimension

Strategic evaluation of the external marketplace is critical because it helps you understand what kind of strategy you should implement. You don't "make up" a strategy; you and your team *decide* on a strategy that will put your company in a unique and valuable position through 3–5 Differentiating Actions.

Now, careful readers out there may be thinking, "Wait a minute, Shannon! Didn't you say earlier that I should write out my strategy regardless of whether it's good, bad, or ugly?"

Yes, I did say that, and I'm glad you've completed that essential first step (and if you haven't done it yet, do it now!). But the first thing you write down is not necessarily the strategy you're going to end up with. Think of that as your rough sketch—a draft—that will forever evolve as your company and the market progress.

---

3 Frank Holmes, "These are the 7 Biggest US Airlines," *Business Insider*, April 6, 2016, http://www.businessinsider.com/these-are-the-7-biggest-us-airlines-2016-4/#7-spirit-1.

Once you write your 3HAG, you and your team now have to validate your 3HAG—your strategy—by putting it into action and continuing to evolve it to best serve your company.

The Attribution Framework

The Attribution Framework will allow you to see how you can position your company to serve the needs of your Core Customer. We've already established that you can't compete on one activity alone. According to Michael Porter's research, there are three generally accepted ways to create a differentiated strategic position:

- Serve the broad needs of a few customers

- Serve some needs of many customers

- Serve many needs for many customers in a super-specific market

We'll now use the Attribution Framework to see where the white space is in your marketplace. Expect this analysis to drive great discussion with your team about how to keep or move your company to the white space—that unique and valuable place in the market. This is one of my favorite tools—the one that creates the most "Aha!" moments when I work with my clients. To download it, go to http://www.shannonsusko.com/.

Do the following with your team:

1. Break your leadership team into groups of three to four people.

2. Have each group take a copy of the tool to work with.

3. Have each group discuss the six to eight key attributes of the market your company is playing. Fill them in on the left-hand side in the column marked "Attributes."

Attribution Framework

Step 1. What are the attributes of your target market?					
Step 2. Rank on a scale of 1 to 5?					
Attributes	Comp 1:	Comp 2:	Comp 3:	Comp 4:	Your Company

4. As a group, go to the column labeled "Your Company" and rank on a scale of 1 to 5 how well your company serves each of these attributes—one by one. Be as honest and realistic as possible. You cannot be good at them all.

5. Now identify three or four competitors. Put the name of a competitor in each of the columns labeled "Comp 1," "Comp 2," and so on. Then do the same ranking for up to four of your competitors.

Attribution Framework Example: Paradata

	Comp1	Comp 2	Paradata
Back Office	3	5	2
Set up	1	2	3
Multi-currency	1	2	3
POS Integration	1	4	1
24/7 Service	3	5	5
Reseller Program	3	1	4
Merchant Accounts	2	2	1

6. Once you have all the competitors ranked, as well as your own company, go to the second page and write the attributes across the bottom axis in the order of best to worst ranking based on *your* company's rankings. In the Paradata example, we would write 24/7 Service as the first attribute across the bottom axis, and then Reseller Program, Setup, Multicurrency, and so on.

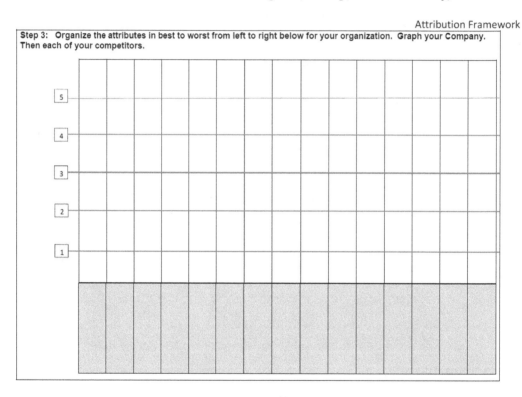

Attribution Framework

Step 3: Organize the attributes in best to worst from left to right below for your organization. **Graph your Company.** Then each of your competitors.

7. Once each group has written the attributes across the bottom axis, plot the line for your company and then for each of your competitors. See Paradata's example below.

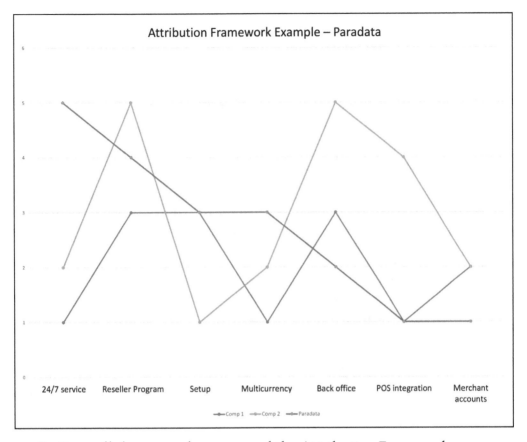

Attribution Framework Example – Paradata

8. Once all the groups have mapped the Attribution Framework, have each group share their graph and how they came up with the results.

9. As a group, decide on what the 6–8 attributes will be for the company. And then have a volunteer collate the input into one graph for the next meeting and post it on the wall of your meeting room.

(Note: There is one more step. Read on and look for step 10. This is your 3HAG Line.)

At Paradata we mapped the attributes that mattered for the payment-processing service provider market. These attributes included setup time, back-office management, payment processors, multicurrency, fees, point-of-sale integration, 24/7 service, and a reseller program.

We rated how Paradata delivered on these attributes. This forces you to do an honest rating of your own company. You cannot be good at everything.

Next, we selected two competitors and ranked how they dealt with those same attributes. Even though there's room on the chart for three or four competitors, focus on the top two in your marketplace unless there are four really solid competitors.

When you're ranking your company, focus on what your team is good at *today*, even if you plan to improve in the near future. If you don't work with where you are at this moment, then your ranking is aspirational, and it won't help you craft your 3HAG.

Based on these results, our team at Paradata saw the areas in which we could excel relative to our competitors: setting up clients, working in multiple currencies, offering 24/7 service, and providing an excellent reseller program. Through this analysis we also decided to put less emphasis on providing merchant accounts and point-of-sale integration.

In making these decisions and strategic trade-offs, we were focusing on the attributes of the market that our Core Customer, Peter, needed. The other two competitors were not serving Peter, and that put us in a unique and valuable position—on our own dimension. As you can see on the top left of the graph, we had this white space all to ourselves. Bingo!

Now it's your turn.

One important realization that often arises during this analysis is that team members may not know all that much about their competitors. In successful high-growth companies everyone on the leadership team should be a market expert. Remember, in our definition of strategy—creating a unique and valuable position in the marketplace—you're not competing *directly* against your competitors. You are competing to be *unique in the marketplace*. And being unique in your marketplace requires a sophisticated understanding of what your market actually looks like. Members of the leadership team of any company must be market experts who are continually studying and keeping their knowledge up to date.

After completing their first Attribution Framework, companies usually step back and say one of two things. Some say, "This shows that we're in the right position. Let's keep the momentum going! Let's keep evolving to remain unique and valuable!"

More often, though, the realization sounds more like this: "Wow! We look like everyone else—and look at all that available white space! We need to evolve our strategy!"

Where Do You Want to Be?

If you've completed your Attribution Framework and, like many companies, have concluded that you're not quite where you want to be, it's time to decide where you really *do* want to be. In the table that you completed above, add a new column to describe how you want your company to meet the attributes of the market. Decide where you will serve the Core Customer well and where you will not. Then add this aspirational line to your Attribution Framework: this is your future unique and valuable position!

Attribution Framework Example: Paradata – 3HAG LINE

	Comp1	Comp 2	Paradata	3HAG Paradata
24/7 Service	1	2	5	5
Reseller Program	3	5	4	5
Set up	3	1	3	5
Multi-currency	1	2	3	5
Back Office	3	5	2	3
POS Integration	1	4	1	2
Merchant Accounts	2	2	1	1

At Paradata, when we first came up with the 3HAG line, it was taking us thirty days to set up a client and we could only process Canadian and US dollars. By using the Attribution Framework, we saw that we could move into our own valuable position if we achieved the following: set up a client in less than an hour, process multiple currencies, always answer the phone (but offer a payment service so good that the phone never rang), support existing merchant account providers, and make it easy for them to sell and to directly support their merchants.

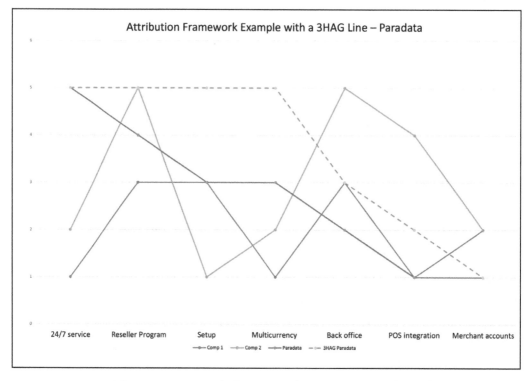

When we mapped these attributes, we saw that we did not have these capabilities at all. But we could see that these interdependent differentiating actions would put us in a unique and valuable space that no other company was serving.

10. The last step is to have a team discussion based on the white space available, what your company should decide to do, and what they should decide not to do. At Paradata we decided to offer 24/7 phone service, a white label Reseller Program, merchant

setup in an hour or less, and multicurrency. In the graph, Paradata's red, dotted 3HAG Line shows what we decided to do to move ourselves into a unique and valuable position. This was aspirational when we plotted it, and we knew we would have to work hard, quarter over quarter, to implement it while keeping a close analytical eye on the market and our company.

Your 3–5 Differentiating Actions

Review your company's Attribution Framework graph with the aspirational 3HAG Line that puts you in the white space. Have a good, full discussion with your team in order to determine the key activities/capabilities that your company will need in order to put you in that white space that you outline in the attributes. Paradata identified the differentiating actions outlined above based on the white space we identified for our 3HAG Line in the Attribution Framework. Once you've identified, discussed, and decided on those differentiating actions as a team, draw each one in a circle on a large sheet of easel paper or on a whiteboard. When building this with your team you may come up with between three and eight actions. Best practice is to whittle this down to three to five in order to keep focus and really carve out your position.

3–5 Differentiating Actions Example – Paradata

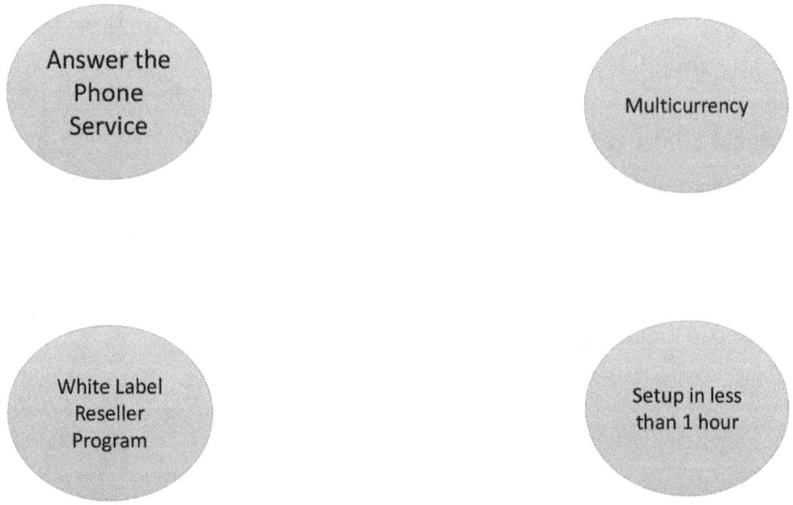

Answer the Phone Service

Multicurrency

White Label Reseller Program

Setup in less than 1 hour

You have just begun what Michael Porter calls the Activity Fit Map. Now that you've determined your differentiating actions, we should add which differentiating actions are dependent on others, as shown above in Paradata's example.

Activity Fit Map I – 3–5 Differentiating Actions – Example – Paradata

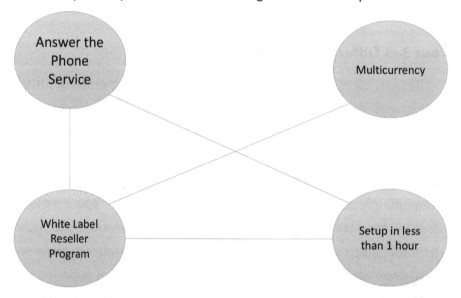

Once most companies have this picture up on the wall, the leadership team is eager to put more detail in the picture to provide more clarity. So the next step is to fill in the tactical activities that will actually put those capabilities in place. In this way, the Activity Fit Map will show you exactly where your company needs to develop in order to move the company toward your 3HAG.

At Paradata it was time to map our four differentiating actions on an Activity Fit Map and determine the supportive activities that would be necessary for each of those four actions. These were our four differentiating actions:

- Setup in less than an hour
- Answer the phones 24/7
- Support any currency
- White label Reseller Program

The picture below is Paradata's Activity Fit Map—what I call Level II. The smaller blue circles show the supporting activities that Paradata would have to perform in order to ensure that we would differentiate ourselves in the four ways specified in the green circles.

Activity Fit Map II – 3–5 Differentiating Actions – Example – Paradata

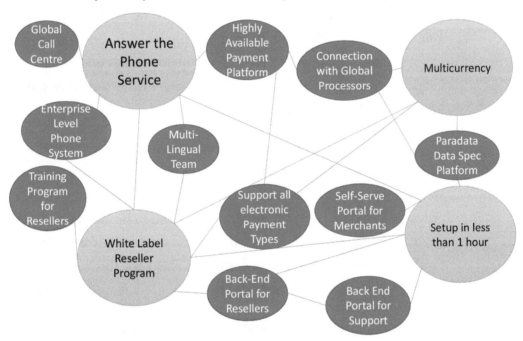

Thanks to this Activity Fit Map, we now saw all the tactical moves that would be necessary to put us in a unique and valuable position. This map became a key Strategic Picture that helped keep us on track. We would use it to better define the twelve quarter-over-quarter march that will be shown in our "Swimlanes," which we'll talk about in more detail shortly.

Put Your Strategy into One Word or Phrase

At Subserveo we summarized our strategy in a single phrase: *Make Compliance Easy.* Why put your strategy into one word or phrase? Because it makes your strategy relatable to everyone in the company and helps everyone focus on what's most important to the

Core Customer and your company. Subserveo team members kept this one-phrase strategy at the top of their minds all the time so that we could continually make good decisions that were consistent with our overall goals. That helped us to maintain our unique and valuable position even as competitors tried to enter our dimension.

In order for your pictures and strategy to be memorable, I want you to be able to distill them into one phrase. Yes, one phrase—so when you are in the thick of it in your business, this one phrase will keep you and your team focused. Everyone in the company should know your One-Phrase Strategy.

At Paradata our One-Phrase Strategy was "Make Payments Easy." This phrase was meaningful to the Paradata team, as this was how we made money; this tied all our differentiating actions together. In order for Paradata to be successful, we needed to be able to make the payment process easy for the whole value chain—but most importantly for resellers and their merchants. This kept the foundation of our strategy intact and drove us to make focused decisions every day.

You will notice that Paradata's One-Phrase Strategy came from the answer to the question raised in our discussion as a leadership team when we gutted out "What do we want to be known for in three years' time?" Take a look at what your team gutted out when they answered this question.

Your One-Phrase Strategy should be a phrase that pulls your 3–5 Differentiating Actions together and is easy to remember and meaningful to the team. When I work with teams at this point, I ask each leader to write down what they think on a sticky note and share it. Sometimes we find one right away that resonates and other times it takes a little longer. At Paradata we put ours right in the middle of the Activity Fit Map.

Activity Fit Map II – ONE PHRASE STRATEGY – Example – Paradata

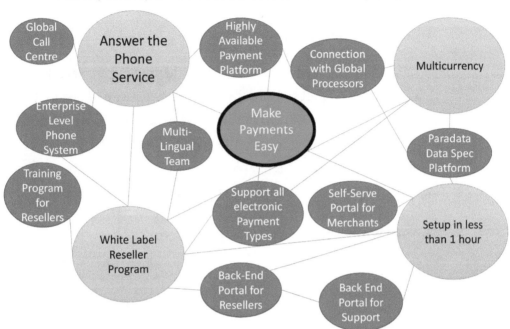

Since you're still near the start of your 3HAG journey, it's not essential that you immediately try to put your company's strategy into a single word or phrase. Just keep it in mind as a powerful tool to bring into play once your team has jointly gutted out your 3HAG and other Strategic Pictures. You'll get to a point where writing out your One-Phrase Strategy will no longer seem like a daunting task; it may just come to you! If you are keen to gut one out, I recommend the following process:

1. Break the leadership team into groups of two. Hand out pads of sticky notes and markers to each group.

2. Ask each group to come up with a One-Phrase Strategy to share with the team.

3. Have each group present to the team what they think the One-Phrase Strategy should be and post it on the whiteboard or easel.

4. Now have the group review and discuss all that are presented and choose a single One-Phrase Strategy—or the top two—and get a volunteer to write them down for the next meeting.

One-Phrase Strategy phrases take a little time to percolate. It's good to write one down but test it out with the whole team to ensure that it creates the "picture"—the alignment and behavior you want from the team. In the beginning, we used this with the leadership team and let it percolate with us; then we shared the 3HAG story with our team and backed it up with our One-Phrase Strategy, which made it much clearer.

Should You Keep Your Strategy a Secret?

No.

Let's go back to the example of Southwest. Everyone knows Southwest's strategy. It's been the subject of many studies, and anyone can read about it. But nobody has successfully copied it in North America. Other companies have tried and failed. Indeed, people have lost their jobs trying to copy Southwest's strategy.

If you have a great strategy, if you've nailed down the three to five differentiating actions that drive your unique and valuable position, then being forthcoming about your strategy isn't going to hurt you. If you have *confidence in your strategy*—thanks to the fact that your position is solid—there's no reason not to talk to your competitors.

In fact, getting to know your competitors and learning what they're doing is valuable for both you and them. There's no need to think of your competitors as the enemy; remember, you're going after a different space in the market than they are. That's the very essence of your unique and valuable position. Being able to get on the phone and call a CEO of a competing organization to say, "We're doing this, you're doing that, and we're going to coexist," means that you've got confidence in your business position.

Companies that lack a great strategy or fail to take differentiating actions tend to be the most secretive and adversarial. They often claim that their greatness is some kind of secret. That's usually a smoke screen to deflect attention from the fact that they have no differentiating actions and there is no secret to their success.

In Subserveo's case, only three companies operated in the post-trade compliance broker-dealer marketplace; Subserveo was one of those three. Our competitors were not friendly with one another, mostly because they were doing exactly the same thing. Subserveo was different, so we didn't get caught up in the infighting. This might sound counterintuitive, but if you want to confirm that you've found your white space, go and talk to your competitors. You'll find out right away how they view your position in the market.

If your competitor is out to get you, first they'll try to match all your differentiating actions. That's what happened at Paradata. Our competitors matched us on our setup times, and then they said that they offered 24/7 on-call phone service. In fact, their phone service was still automated, but they claimed to have matched us. Basically, they came at us by attacking the low-hanging fruit—those differentiating actions that were not core to our existence. Our competitors could not map data as quickly and securely as we could, and it was very difficult for them to execute any of our four differentiating actions as well as Paradata. Our competitors eventually discovered that it would require quite a bit of time and money to do what we did, and the easier solution was to buy us out—which is exactly what happened.

Speeding Forward

Take a moment to acknowledge how much progress you've made since the start of this book. You have defined your core values and Core Purpose. You've gutted out your first-ever 3HAG, as well as the 10-to-30-year goal—your BHAG. You've also discovered where your white space is: that open area in the market where your company will carve out its unique and valuable position. And to move you still closer to that unique and valuable position, you've decided upon your 3–5 Differentiating Actions shown in your Activity Fit Map; these are exactly the capabilities your company needs to develop. There may have been a time when your company was driving around the block, but now you're accelerating forward!

In the next chapter, we're going to talk about the confidence you need for pursuing your 3HAG in a steady, quarter-over-quarter approach, even as you make adjustments along the way.

Check-in

1. Gut out your first 3HAG ✓

2. Create your Key Process Flow Map ✓

3. Create your Market Map ✓

4. Define your Core Customer ✓

5. Create your Attribution Framework ✓

6. Name your 3–5 Differentiating Actions by completing your Activity Fit Map ✓

7. Draw your Activity Fit Map II ✓

8. Summarize your One-Phrase Strategy ✓

9. Gut out your Swimlanes

CHAPTER TAKEAWAYS

✔ Use the Attribution Framework to find your market's white space.

✔ Use the Activity Fit Map to map out the 3–5 Differentiating Actions that your company will take to put itself in its unique and valuable position, and the strategic activities that your company will need to perform in order to achieve those differentiating actions.

The Strategic Execution System that Ensures Your Strategy Is Not a Wild-Ass-Guess!

✔ Summarize your One-Phrase Strategy to keep your team focused
  on where you are heading.

Chapter 7

Swimlanes: When You Know Where You're Going, You Know You're Great

Confidence is contagious. So is lack of confidence.
—Vince Lombardi

We've covered a lot of ground, but we're not done yet! This chapter is about the power of knowing exactly where you're going.

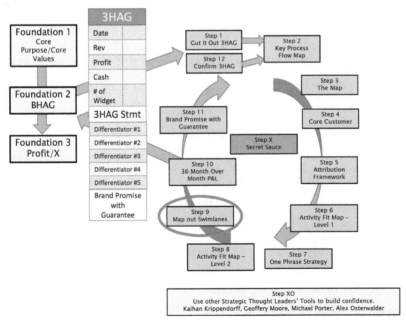

Of all the companies I've worked with over the years, there isn't one that didn't have a moment of clarity at this point in this process. We've mapped out the marketplace, and we've determined what the company's unique and valuable position will be within that marketplace. We've mapped the company internally and established who its Core Customer is, and we have a view of where it's positioned among its competitors. This work gives the leadership team a clear perspective on the company's present and future, bringing a powerful sense of clarity that was previously lacking.

That clarity in turn creates confidence, and that confidence influences your whole team. Since strategic execution planning is an iterative process, you get better and sharper each time you convene back in your war room, and everyone feels the power of being confident about the company's direction. But don't stop here. The next two steps in the 3HAG framework are the most important. Most companies are very proud to get to this point; they have so much more clarity than they did when they started and do not put deliberate effort into the next two steps. This is where we ensure your company reaches your 3HAG—whatever it is. I cannot stress this enough—*keep on moving forward in the 3HAG journey.*

As I've already mentioned, I was able to sell my second company, Subserveo, quickly precisely because we had accurately predicted in our first quarter where we were going to be in quarter twelve, thirty-six months away. Being able to predict where we would be three years out and then advancing, quarter over quarter, to that goal showed our buyers that we knew where we should be headed that was unique and valuable and we could execute the steps needed to make our 3HAG a reality. Now *that's* the goose that lays the golden eggs. I want this for your company too.

Indeed, those accurate predictions sent our company's valuation through the roof. Buyers like predictability, teams like predictability, people like predictability. And predictability feeds directly into team confidence.

With all of this important strategic work already under your belt—keeping in mind that the 3HAG is a repeatable, iterative process—it's time to go deeper into the concept of "Swimlanes." It's time to get into the guts of your twelve quarter-over-quarter plan and 36 Month Rolling Forecast.

Strategic Execution: How to March Forward

The purpose of the 3HAG framework is not only to get you to define a unique and differentiated position for your company and foster the confidence that goes along with that; I also want you to have a 3HAG so you can easily explain the *how*: how exactly you're going to execute on that strategy now through the next twelve quarters.

3HAG – Strategic Execution System

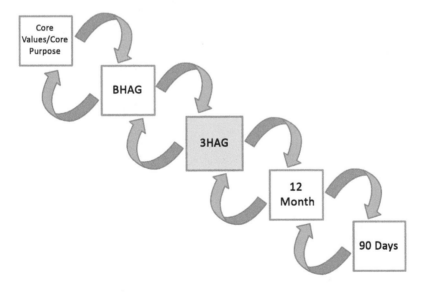

At Paradata we felt a strong sense of urgency to define a strategy that would take us three years into the future. To do that, we realized that we had to build a quarter-over-quarter plan to give ourselves confidence that we really would achieve the outcome in our plan. Then we were able to share that plan—and that confidence—with all of our stakeholders, including our board of directors and investors.

Indeed, the sense of urgency created by our board of directors, in which we absolutely *had* to get clear on our strategy tied to our 3HAG, and then deliver on it, quarter over quarter, created the right conditions for success. *Every* company should hold itself to these same rules, rather than the much more common approach of operating with a static strategy that does not have a clear quarter-over-quarter plan beyond four quarters.

So now let's turn to what we called the Swimlanes: exactly how you're going to get where you want to go. This is the true gold of the 3HAG. It's also the hardest part. Go figure.

A lot of companies are satisfied with the clarity they have received to date and do not take these next steps. *Do not be one of these companies!* If you really want to achieve your 3HAG, your team needs to focus and build out your 3HAG Swimlanes and 36 Month, month-over-month Rolling Forecast.

3HAG

| Date |
| Rev |
| Profit |
| Cash |
| # of Widgets |

3HAG Stmt

| Differentiator #1 |
| Differentiator #2 |
| Differentiator #3 |
| Differentiator #4 |
| Differentiator #5 |
| Brand Promise with Guarantee |

SWIMLANES

Q12	Q11	Q10	Q9	Q8	Q7	Q6	Q5	Q4	Q3	Q2	Q1

1HAG

| Date |
| Rev |
| Profit |
| Cash |
| # of Widgets |

1HAG Stmt

| Company Priority #1 |
| Company Priority #2 |
| Company Priority #3 |
| Company Priority #4 |
| Company Priority #5 |
| Critical # of Widgets |

In the last chapter you determined the 3–5 Differentiating Actions that will put your company in a unique and valuable position. This is great. Now we want to ensure you get to that position. This is where the Swimlanes comes in.

If you search "Swimlanes" on Google the search engine will come up with a lot of project management process and jargon. When we came up with this idea, we realized that our large three-year development projects always had Swimlanes, and we ran ninety-day sprints. Why would we not do this with the biggest and riskiest project that we would ever face—our company? So the leadership team got together and took each of the four differentiators and mapped out what it would look like to go from where we were today, quarter over quarter for twelve quarters, capturing the major milestones and assumptions. We then created a six-row by twelve-column grid on a wall and got some large sticky notes. Each row was a Swimlane for one of our differentiators; and in each quarter, we added in the key milestones on a sticky note. We lined this all up for all four differentiators. Wow, what a view! We now could see the whole path—the good, the bad, and the ugly.

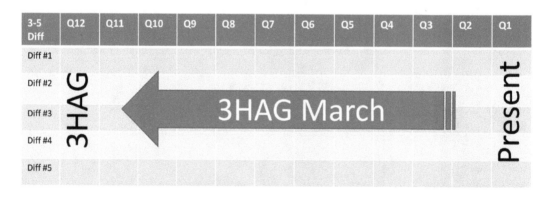

The discussion from that point was looking horizontally across the quarters and vertically to see where we had dependencies, too many or too few resources, and the assumptions aligned with all the milestones. This is such a key point in time for your 3HAG. Do not skip this step.

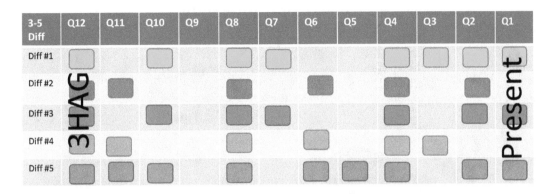

The 3–5 Differentiating Actions are Key Capabilities that you will have in place at the end of the three years—Q12, or Quarter 12. You will be celebrating with your team when you achieve your fiscal goals because you deliberately put these capabilities in place.

We'll use Paradata as an example of how to start planning your Swimlanes. In our 3HAG, the outcome in year 3 was the following:

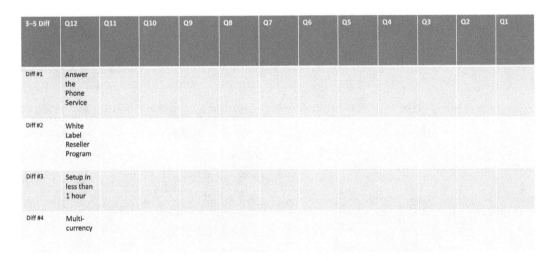

Paradata's Activity Fit Map II is shown below. This is a key step to getting more granular on how you are going to achieve these differentiating actions. It really helps get the whole team involved.

Activity Fit Map II – 3–5 Differentiating Actions – Example – Paradata

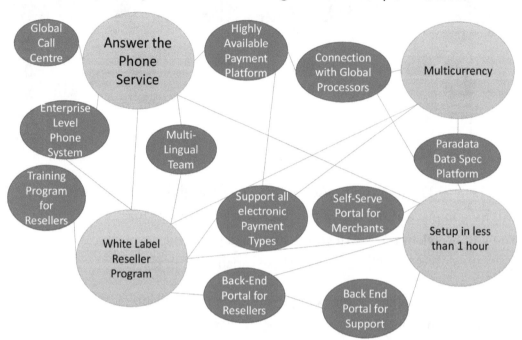

The Activity Fit Map II allows you to start laying out what should go in your Swimlanes and also challenge the ideas in your Activity Fit Map, as the smaller circles are more tactical and usually end up as quarterly milestones in your Swimlanes. Below is the first draft of Paradata's Swimlanes with the smaller circles mapped to the quarters in which they needed to be delivered. This is a great way to get your full team into a great discussion and ultimately to understand how you're going to get where you want to go—to agree, disagree, discuss, and finalize an agreement on a path forward. Everyone is looking at the same Swimlane. This is so powerful!

Each month and each quarter we filled in our Swimlanes by pinning down the necessary milestones associated with each differentiating action. In this case, the milestone was ensuring that our customers got set up and were able to use our product as quickly as possible. In other words, what milestones did we need to hit in order to move the company forward, make great and quick decisions for today, and

3–5 Diff	Q12	Q11	Q10	Q9	Q8	Q7	Q6	Q5	Q4	Q3	Q2	Q1
Diff #1	Answer the Phone Service		Global Call Centre				Multi-Lingual Team		Enterprise Level Phone System			Human Answers the Phone
Diff #2	White Label Reseller Program				Back-End Portal for Resellers	EU Reseller	5 X USA ISO Resells	Training Program for Resellers	Support for all payment types	USA ISO Resells	Highly Available Payment Platform	CAD Bank Resells
Diff #3	Setup in less than 1 hour		4 hours		1 days		7 days	Self-Serve Portal for Merchants	30 days	Back-End Portal for Support	Paradata Data Spec Platform	60 days
Diff #4	Multi-currency	Global Processor X 1	Global Processor X 1	Global Processor X 1	Global Processor X 1	Global Processor X 1	Global Processor X 1	Global Processor X 1	Global Processor X 1	Global Processor X 1	USA Processor X 1	Canada Processor X 1

build our confidence that we were headed in the right direction? We brainstormed and wrote the milestones into the appropriate lane on the wall of our war room.

We also specified necessary milestones by looking at the trends we saw in the marketplace. Remember when we mapped out the marketplace in chapter 4? This is a place where that map comes in very handy. You've already analyzed what's happening externally; now use that map to tailor your Swimlanes to what you want to achieve each year relative to what's going on in the environment around you.

Next, it's time for you to do the same with your team. Take your Activity Fit Map II, find a whiteboard, put masking tape on a wall, or use easel paper taped together to create your Swimlanes and start filling them in with the smaller support circles from your Activity Fit Map.

After this step I often get asked who is accountable for each Swimlane. This is a team, of course, and a Team Goal—so who should be accountable? With our Paradata team, the Swimlanes were our Team Goal, and for each milestone in the Swimlane, someone volunteered to be accountable. This worked great. In each of our Swimlanes there were multiple function owners who had to contribute in order to achieve the Key Differentiator we set out to accomplish.

I have worked with other companies over the years that have had functional owners *own* a Key Differentiator. This has worked fine, too. What I have observed is that for a larger company, the latter works best, and for a smaller company, the former works best. Either method will get the success you want as long as the Swimlanes remain on the monthly and quarterly agendas of your planning meetings.

Once you have created the Swimlanes, they are "alive" and will now need to evolve as the market evolves and as your company evolves.

This is an amazing view. If I have not said it enough—build out your Swimlanes now.

I want to pause for a moment and acknowledge the practical difficulty in what you're doing in your Swimlanes. In a sense, I'm asking you to predict the future. I'm not suggesting that this is easy! What I want you to do is write it down and share so you can start making progress toward your 3HAG.

Indeed, the work of filling out your Swimlanes is very challenging. And as an additional complicating factor, no one wants to be wrong. Your team members want to be confident in their predictions. They want to "guess" correctly, and that's only human. But it's crucial that you not let this inhibit your forward movement. Openly acknowledge that everyone is doing their best to craft accurate, highly achievable targets and that you won't be correct 100 percent of the time. (And yet, as you get better and better at this, and at executing on each stated milestone, you may find that you're right a lot more than you would have thought!)

At Paradata, my team and I wanted to be right—that's why we developed the Swimlanes in the first place. This was an easy way to map out what we needed to do and discuss how it would be done. That meant that, in very practical terms, we were more likely to predict correctly and hit our goals, because we had formed those predictions and goals on the foundation of really solid strategic planning work.

We updated our Swimlanes frequently—at a minimum every quarter, as our external analysis (Market Map) and our internal analysis (Key Process Flow Map), continued to evolve. This is an important point. We had to ensure that our twelve-quarter Swimlane milestones and forecast kept evolving as the company developed. In order to ensure this evolution was taking place, we held a monthly leadership team meeting to review the 36 Month Rolling Forecast (which I will explain in the next chapter), where we made any adjustments required to the key milestones in our Swimlanes.

How Do Swimlanes Fit In with Your 1HAG/Annual Plan?

As I have mentioned many times, this not your traditional planning process where you will create an Annual Plan and then only have that visibility as you are getting closer to the end of the year and nothing beyond. The idea behind the Swimlanes was to get granular on how to move forward for the next four quarters and the eight quarters beyond that. You can see what Swimlanes look like using Verne Harnish's One-Page Strategic Plan format—which I am a big fan of—on the next page.

You can see that there are still twelve quarters of Swimlanes, and we just created our 1HAG, or Annual Plan, with company priorities that we will end up with in twelve months' time. This process and continuity of this process make monthly, quarterly, and annual planning a lot less difficult because you will be looking at this plan continuously.

You Can Reach Out and Touch It

The whole reason we chose the 3 in 3HAG and named it the "3 Year Highly Achievable Goal" is that three years is close enough that you can reach out and touch it.

But the *how* is crucial: How are you going to get where you want to go? And that's where the Swimlanes come into play. This gives you a specific, achievable road map so you know just where you're going. Most important, your team believes in it. They make decisions and take actions every day to move toward it. They feel the momentum, and they see the endgame. That kind of confidence is infectious. And marrying this with a 36 Month, month-over-month Rolling Forecast (which you'll find in the next chapter) is the key to continue building on your team's confidence.

The Strategic Execution System that Ensures Your Strategy Is Not a Wild-Ass-Guess!

1HAG

Date	
Rev	
Profit	
Cash	
# of Widgets	

3HAG

Date	
Rev	
Profit	
Cash	
# of Widgets	

SWIMLANES — Q4 Q3 Q2 Q1

SWIMLANES — Q12 Q11 Q10 Q9 Q8 Q7 Q6 Q5

1HAG Stmt

- Company Priority #1
- Company Priority #2
- Company Priority #3
- Company Priority #4
- Company Priority #5
- Critical # of Widgets

3HAG Stmt

- Differentiator #1
- Differentiator #2
- Differentiator #3
- Differentiator #4
- Differentiator #5
- Brand Promise with Guarantee

Check-in

1. Gut out your first 3HAG ✓
2. Create your Key Process Flow Map ✓
3. Create your Market Map ✓
4. Define your Core Customer ✓
5. Create your Attribution Framework ✓
6. Name your 3–5 Differentiating Actions by completing your Activity Fit Map ✓
7. Draw your Activity Fit Map II ✓
8. Summarize your One-Phrase Strategy ✓
9. Gut out your Swimlanes ✓
10. Develop your 36 Month, month-over-month Rolling Forecast that aligns with your Swimlanes

CHAPTER TAKEAWAYS

✔ The purpose of the 3HAG framework is not only to get you to define a unique and differentiated position for your company but also to foster the confidence that goes along with such a rock-solid plan.

✔ In order to develop such confidence, you've got to work with your leadership team to map out—quarter by quarter—how to achieve each of your 3–5 Differentiating Actions.

✔ You gutted-out your Swimlanes!

Chapter 8

36 Month Rolling Forecast: Roll It Forward and Never Stop

In business, what's dangerous is not to evolve.
—Jeff Bezos

M ost companies have a twelve-month "budget." This is a word that I never use or say, and it's unlikely you'll see it again in this book after this chapter. A budget is a license to spend regardless of what you are achieving on your topline. I've seen teams continue to spend money, not for the company goal but because they don't want to lose their budget dollars for next year; they know if they don't spend it all this year they won't get the same amount next year. I have also seen teams continue to spend what is in their budget because they think they are on plan and know no differently and carry on. They don't have the information to know that they should not spend because they are off plan, or they should spend sooner because they are way ahead of plan. This behavior is absolutely opposite to focusing on the overall company, where we only want to spend what we can afford and what makes sense to achieve our goals.

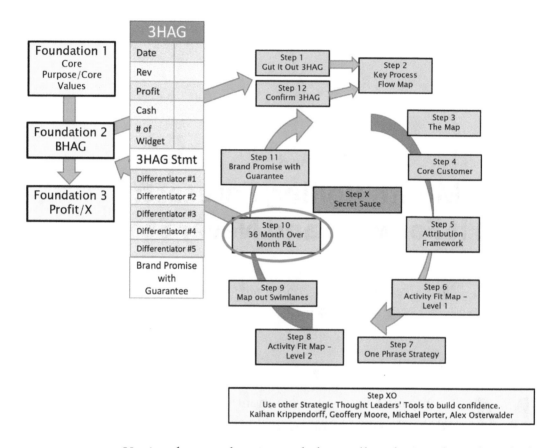

You're about to learn a tool that will make you lose the whole budget concept forever. My team at Paradata developed the 36 Month, month-over-month Rolling Forecast to increase our confidence as leaders by specifying exactly what we needed to do to reach our 3HAG. When we shared our three-year forecast with the board of directors, we wanted to feel confident, and we wanted to ensure that every board meeting going forward, we would be just as confident and that the leadership team was totally clear on how we were going to achieve our fiscal goals and be held accountable for those goals.

Paradata was a subscription-based business. Because of that, if we missed any quarter, any month, or any week in our forecast, it was very hard to make it up later and still achieve our 3HAG. So, we decided to forecast, month over month, how much cash we wanted in the bank at the end of each month. Yes—CASH! We then forecast our expenses and then our revenue, and then we worked our way back down by starting with the "widgets"—in this case, the new merchants—we were going to add to the platform each month. In order to forecast this, we used our Swimlanes and assumptions to come up with the new merchant numbers, where these new merchants would come from, and so on. Then we calculated revenue and the expenses that would be necessary to serve those merchants and build our company for the future. Finally, we looked at our profit and cash.

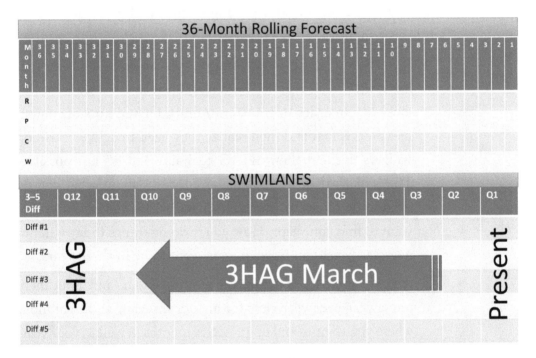

This looks scary. It probably sounds like a lot. But I can tell you that the curiosity that this process piques in your leadership team is absolutely amazing, worthwhile, and confidence-building for clarity and believability of your 3HAG. It inspires the exact conversation you want to be having regarding accountability and ownership of the revenue, expenses, profit, and cash.

And just to be crystal clear, this tool is not solely for your finance team. Finance can set up the model that the rest of the leadership team will contribute to significantly.

How Do You Get Started?

The most important thing is to just *start*. Lots of teams avoid this step. Don't be one of them. You have come this far—you have your Swimlanes up on the wall and you have already gutted out your fiscal year-ending numbers for your 3HAG; let's validate them now that we have spent time on your Swimlanes seriously mapping this out. Your probability of hitting your 3HAG will decrease if you skip this.

Here are your options for getting started with your 36 Month, month-over-month Rolling Forecast:

1. If you have a twelve-month budget, you can take it and extrapolate it with some assumed percentage increases and see what this looks like in order to get to your draft 3HAG. Lots of companies do this first and then realize they need to deliver a trillion widgets to meet their 3HAG goal and that it's not possible. That's okay; this process creates curiosity about what you do need to do to get to your 3HAG and where the gaps are. You want to find your gaps. How you're doing things today will not necessarily get you to where you want to be in three years.

2. Another approach is to take the past three years and input them into a year-over-year view for historical review and then input where you want to end up in twelve months as well as your year-three target from your gutted-out 3HAG; then look at year two and fill it in. Again, this will drive an incredible conversation at the leadership team table about how you'll get to your 3HAG. That's exactly what you want. And the more the team digs in, the more they'll want to dig into this. Then build this out into a 36 Month, month-over-month Rolling Forecast. (Visit http://www.shannonsusko.com/ to download the worksheet.)

3. Another option is to have the finance team create an Excel model for thirty-six months with a detailed Profit and Loss statement that pulls from many worksheets owned by each individual leader

in their functional area. This is a team approach to forecasting, where the marketing and sales team builds their widget-based forecasts, and the other functional teams build their widget-based assumptions of how to serve this growth. Once again this will drive very detailed planning and discussions, which is exactly what you want to ensure your 3HAG really is highly achievable. (Visit http://www.shannonsusko.com/ to download a template.)

The first two options are great to get a skeptical team going down this forecasting path. Once you get the discussion started you will want to complete option three as well.

After you have your first draft, you'll want to start refining your first twelve months; this should be the twelve months corresponding with the first year in your 3HAG. And this will eventually be the twelve-month plan that you'll get approved by your leadership team, board, and shareholders. This becomes, in a sense, "locked in" as you start the year. (If you're currently in the middle of your fiscal year, don't worry. Just carve out the right number of months between now and the end of your fiscal year. You also might want to consider making this forecast for a little more than thirty-six months. And we are going to roll it forward every month anyway.)

Here are a few key things to keep in mind:

- Your twelve-month forecast gets created, approved, and locked in for the year.

- Every month you review with the leadership team your approved forecast and discuss where you are and what you need to adjust. VERY IMPORTANT: You are adjusting your *Rolling* Forecast— not your approved forecast, but your *Rolling* Forecast.

- Each month you add another month at the end of the forecast, so there are always thirty-six months forecast at any given time, regardless of where you are in the fiscal year.

- When you get to the end of the year and start planning for the next twelve months, as most companies do, you will already have a well-discussed draft of your twelve-month plan for the next year, and it's already aligned with your 3HAG.

36 Month Rolling Forecast

A 36 Month Rolling Forecast usually terrifies leadership teams. Don't let it! This is the GOLD you have been looking for. It's worth digging for it.

You now have an approved forecast, so we're going to create the Rolling Forecast. Here's what you'll need to do:

1. Take the approved forecast—save it as the Rolling Forecast.

2. Add two columns to the left of the approved column for every month —one column will be for the actual results and the other will be for the Rolling Forecast.

Detailed Profit and Loss Statement								
Month 1			Month 2			Month X		
Actual	Rolling	Approved	Actual	Rolling	Approved	Actual	Rolling	Approved
Rev								
Exp								
Profit								
Cash								

When your finance team first creates this model, the Rolling and the Approved will be the same numbers. You will then change the Rolling Forecast to reflect what is happening internally and externally as time elapses. How many times have you gotten halfway through the year and your budget was so far off you just kept changing it, or you just lived with it—and found it utterly demotivating? This happens all the time.

We want to avoid this outcome—not by throwing out what we thought at the beginning of the year, but by acknowledging what we thought, understanding what was different, and evolving the Rolling Forecast to reflect new knowledge and true cash position. This is key!

12 Quarter Forecast of Your Functional Design

In chapter 4, we created a functional design of the organization. In your detailed 36 Month Rolling Forecast, you have created a functional forecast based on the functional positions you need filled. You now have all the information required to forecast your Full-Time Equivalents (FTEs) for each quarter for twelve quarters to your 3HAG. This is important for your whole team to understand and realize, because if they only see the topline and fiscal numbers increasing without the specific increase in resources, your team is less likely to believe in or even want to believe in the plan.

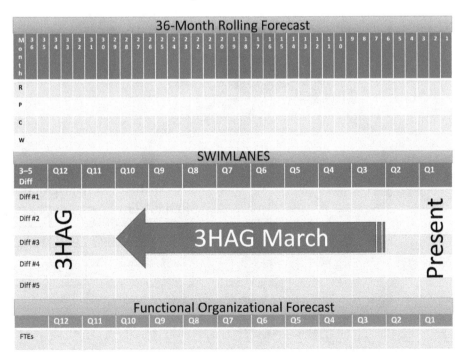

It is a best practice to forecast the functional organizational chart for twelve quarters. This allows the whole team to see what positions will become available and where team members have an opportunity to grow. As well, team members can share with colleagues outside of the firm the upcoming positions, making it easier to fill these positions as they become available. This is a very proactive and valuable approach to building your team to grow with the company.

Swimlanes and Forecasting

Your Swimlanes play an important role in your 36 Month Rolling Forecast. Specifically, the assumptions you made as a team as to when and how you would reach each of the milestones to implementing your 3–5 Differentiating Actions are critical in your 36 Month Rolling Forecast.

Your Swimlanes show the resources—in terms of cash and people— that are required to reach each milestone. Your Swimlanes also show

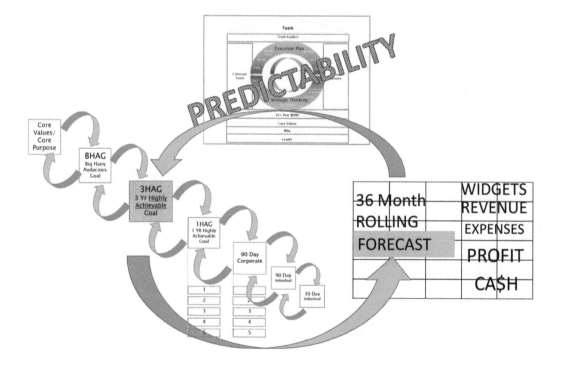

what you need to deliver in each and every quarter. The 36 Month Rolling Forecast and Swimlanes go hand in hand. They never stop "feeding" each other.

This is where your Swimlanes plus your 36 Month Rolling Forecast really take over. From now on, it will be critical to keep these in focus at every meeting.

Recently a company that was using the 3HAG reviewed their last quarter and realized that, due to the market changing, they were less likely to reach their 3HAG. They organized a few key meetings to focus on this market issue so they could put the company back on track. Which they did!

Another company I work with recently met their original 3HAG in fewer than three years. This happens quite often—because when you write down your goal and get your team behind it, they usually find a way to achieve it faster. Pretty fantastic, right?

Why Does Your 3HAG Roll Away from You over Time?

Your 3HAG will become your 2HAG and then your 1HAG.

As you work toward your 3HAG it will get closer and closer. Soon it's fewer than twenty-four months away, then fewer than twelve.

That's why you will create a new 3HAG every year, so that you always have a 3HAG that's three years away. This is a crucial part of achieving your BHAG, your 10-to-30-year goal: You must always have a 3HAG that's three years out. At the same time, the 3HAG from the year you just finished will become your 2HAG, and your 2HAG will become your 1HAG. I have seen teams with 3HAGs that are only twelve months away; this will not help you reach your BHAG. So you will *always* have a 3HAG!

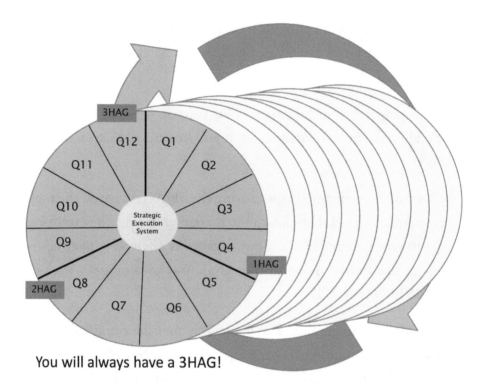

You will always have a 3HAG!

The world is constantly changing—outside of your company as well as within it—so here's a tip for saving yourself headaches. Rather than rewriting your Swimlanes whenever something changes, write each cell of your Swimlane grid on a sticky note. That way you'll easily be able to swap things out and update. Always keep your Swimlane grid on the wall where everyone can see it—preferably in your war room. If it's not visible, it loses the power to guide your team's day-to-day actions.

Your 36 Month, month-over-month Rolling Forecast, aligned with your Swimlanes, isn't static. The two are organic, ever-evolving tools that you adjust as you move forward. They give you a specific, achievable road map so you know just where you're going. Most important, your team believes in it. Your team will make decisions and take actions every day to move toward it. They feel the momentum, and they see the endgame. That kind of confidence is contagious.

And now, with all this hard work under your belt, it's time to explore your Secret Sauce.

Check-in

1. Gut out your first 3HAG ✓

2. Create your Key Process Flow Map ✓

3. Create your Market Map ✓

4. Define your Core Customer ✓

5. Create your Attribution Map ✓

6. Name your 3–5 Differentiating Actions by completing your Activity Fit Map ✓

7. Draw your Activity Fit Map II ✓

8. Summarize your One-Phrase Strategy ✓

9. Gut out your Swimlanes ✓

10. Create your 36 Month, month-over-month Rolling Forecast ✓

11. Determine your Brand Promise with a Guarantee and your Secret Sauce

CHAPTER TAKEAWAYS

✔ Your 36 Month, month-over-month Rolling Forecast is a *leadership team* tool—not a finance team tool. DO NOT pass this on to your CFO and forget about it.

✔ The Twelve Quarter-over-Quarter Functional Organizational Chart is a great way to gain clarity on resources, grow team members, and proactively attract new team members.

Chapter 9

Bring It All Together with a Guaranteed Promise and Secret Sauce

I don't believe in psychology. I believe in good moves.
—Bobby Fischer

W e've now reached the point where the Strategic Pictures and tools we've been creating have all come together to form your 3HAG. This is a huge milestone. And to back up your 3HAG with confidence, we are ready to charge boldly to the next level. We're now going to tackle your differentiated brand promise with a guarantee. This is where we take the information gleaned from all those maps and Strategic Pictures and capitalize on them for market clarity and team alignment for exponential returns.

Brand Promise with a Guarantee

Every company needs a differentiated brand promise with a guarantee. Most companies have a brand promise but do not guarantee the promise made. We want to promise something to our Core Customer that really matters to them, so they will be attracted to our company and buy at a profit.

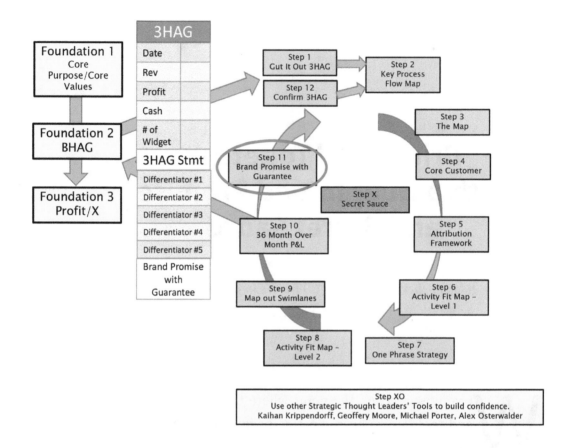

Now that you've figured out who your Core Customer is, and your 3–5 Differentiating Actions and how to deliver on them, you are in a great place to brainstorm and write down your differentiated brand promise with a guarantee.

A *differentiated brand promise with a guarantee* addresses what you and your team believe to be the *greatest need your customers have* and assures those customers that you can solve that problem better than any of your competitors. Your unique brand promise with a guarantee shows your Core Customer how your company stands out from the competition and presents a persuasive argument for why they should purchase goods or services from you rather than from any other company in your marketplace. It offers clarity as to why your Core Customer should do business with your company.

Let's look at a few real-world, highly effective brand promises with guarantees:

- L.L. Bean: "Our products are guaranteed to give 100% satisfaction in every way. Return anything purchased from us at any time if it proves otherwise."

- Orvis: "We will refund your money on any purchase that isn't 100% satisfactory. Anytime, for any reason. It's that simple."

- Eddie Bauer: "Every item we sell will give you complete satisfaction or you may return it for a full refund."

- Costco: "100% satisfaction guaranteed. We guarantee your satisfaction on every product we sell with a full refund. We will refund your membership fee in full at any time if you are dissatisfied."

- OXO: "We guarantee everything we make. If for any reason you are not satisfied with an OXO product, get in touch with us for a replacement or refund."

- Craftsman by Sears: "If this hand tool ever fails to provide complete satisfaction, it will be repaired or replaced free of charge."

As you can see from these brand promises and guarantees, the brand promise with guarantee makes a definite commitment to the customer, and if the company does not deliver on that commitment, then the company will be "hurt" in some way because of it—usually by issuing a refund or a replacement.

The brand promises with a guarantee that you just read are effective because these companies truly deliver on their promises. Empty brand promises with a guarantee or a brand promise without a guarantee mean nothing, no matter how catchy they sound.

Why a Guarantee?

The brand promise with a guarantee is what Jim Collins called "the catalytic mechanism" in his *Harvard Business Review* article "Turning Goals into Results: The Power of Catalytic Mechanisms."[1] Many companies set their BHAG and then have difficulty achieving it. That's why the 3HAG is such a useful framework: the 3HAG is all about linking your goals and differentiated actions to tangible results. This is where Collins's catalytic mechanism comes into play.

Simply put, a catalytic mechanism is an organizational tool for aligning your team behind your Strategic Execution System by empowering each team member to act on behalf of the Core Customer to deliver what matters most. Here are Collins's own words:

> Catalytic mechanisms are the crucial link between objectives and performance; they are a galvanizing, nonbureaucratic means to turn one into the other. Put another way, catalytic mechanisms are to visions what the central elements of the U.S. Constitution are to the Declaration of Independence— devices that translate lofty aspirations into concrete reality. They make big, hairy, audacious goals reachable.[2]

If you've never heard of catalytic mechanisms, you're not alone. In the course of his research on catalytic mechanisms, Jim Collins found that, at most, 10 percent of all companies employed them.[3] And yet, once created, catalytic mechanisms are a critical component for driving companies toward their 3HAGs, and ultimately, their BHAGs.

According to Collins, catalytic mechanisms share five identifiable characteristics:

---

1 Jim Collins, "Turning Goals into Results: The Power of Catalytic Mechanisms," *Harvard Business Review*, July–August 1999, https://hbr.org/1999/07/turning-goals-into-results-the-power-of-catalytic-mechanisms.
2 Collins, *Harvard Business Review*, July–August 1999.
3 Ibid.

1. **Catalytic mechanisms produce *desired results in unpredictable ways.***

   This means you and your team are willing to try unexpected ways of achieving your brand promise—rather than dictating how you're going to achieve your goal.

2. **Catalytic mechanisms distribute power in ways that benefit the entire system, often to the detriment of traditional power players.**

   In traditional business environments, the CEO has the last say on everything. Wielding total control, a CEO can generally get everyone on the team to do just about anything he or she wants. However, this book is about working *together* with your team—a team committed to team results—and this element of creating a catalytic mechanism supports this in a big way. Collins says the catalytic mechanism "subverts the default, knee-jerk tendency of bureaucracies to choose inaction over action, status quo over change, and idiotic rules over common sense."[4] An effective catalytic mechanism shifts the balance of power away from the CEO and leadership team and toward the growth of the company. That's what you're accomplishing every time you have a meeting to discuss your 3HAG: you're dispersing power throughout your team. When everyone is a stakeholder, your company is more likely to succeed.

3. **Catalytic mechanisms can hurt your competitors *or* your own company.**

   This is the "hurt" of a catalytic mechanism. Walk the walk: whatever your brand guarantee is, back it up with action. Catalytic mechanisms have an internal impact, too: In order to achieve your company's goal, the catalytic mechanism must be directly tied to team member performance. For example, if the company

---

4 Ibid.

fails to meet its goals and priorities, some companies may dock pay or not realize their performance compensation—for everyone, including C-suite folks. Knowing that their personal income is at stake could make all the difference between a lackadaisical, inert team and an active, engaged one.

4. **Catalytic mechanisms encourage the departure of team members who don't agree with the company's strategy and goals.**
   In a traditional company setting, team members will often "go with the flow" even if they're not totally on board with the company's purpose, core values, and BHAG. Catalytic mechanisms encourage people who don't share your team's core values to leave. Notice the word *team*, which we've been using throughout. Some people don't like working on teams or sharing leadership roles. Creating a 3HAG requires everyone to work together for the Team Goals, and people who don't function well in that kind of environment will leave . . . or you'll encourage them to find someplace else, outside the company, where they can thrive. The key to success is having the right people with the right mind-set, doing the right thing for the Core Customer. Having the right skill set isn't enough.

5. **Catalytic mechanisms are enforced all the time.**
   Successful catalytic mechanisms keep on working. There's no expiration date. Amend your catalytic mechanism as necessary, as conditions change, but you should consider it a powerful long-term tool for your company. This is where your strategy and execution put the rubber to the road—this is the core of achieving your 3HAG.

Another way to think of your company's catalytic mechanism is *how you make your brand promise hurt*. L.L. Bean's brand promise is top-quality products; they make that promise "hurt" by guaranteeing a refund to any customer who is not completely satisfied. This "hurt" ensures that the whole company becomes aligned to serve the Core Customer. You've heard the expression "Put your money where your mouth is." That's exactly what a company does by guaranteeing its brand promise.

My second company, Subserveo, was in the business of making it easy for small- to medium-size broker-dealers throughout North America to meet post-trade compliance requirements. Our brand promise was to "make compliance easy." To guarantee that promise, we committed to providing smooth, easy service, and—this is the real "hurt"—if we didn't, our clients could terminate their agreement with Subserveo anytime, no questions asked, with a refund that the customer thought was appropriate.

This guarantee was a huge risk for our company—and that's why it was perfect. The whole team was fully empowered to make our Core Customer happy by serving them in any way necessary in order to deliver a positive, easy experience.

This brand promise made my whole team uncomfortable. As it should have! We were willing to let customers out of service agreements without requiring them to pay an early termination penalty, and if they had paid up front for a whole year, we would refund their full payment, which meant we would lose recurring revenue. If this happened regularly, it would hurt our revenue and long-term growth, or even put us out of business.

With this possibility constantly in the back of their minds, the team was focused on delivering excellent customer service all the time. It worked. We never had to pay out on this guarantee. We were operationally aligned with our strategy, our 3HAG, which empowered our team to act on our promise.

Your Company's Brand Promise with a Guarantee

Now let's take a stab at formulating a brand promise with a guarantee for *your* company.

Believe it or not, you've already mapped out your company's differentiated brand promise through the definition of your Core Customer and your differentiating actions. Take a minute to review your detailed description of your Core Customer and your Activity Fit Map from chapter 6, and your answer to the following question from your gutted-out 3HAG: "What do you want your company to be known for in three years' time?"

You're going to use this material to formulate a short brand promise with a guarantee that spells out your commitment to your Core Customer and your guarantee that you're going to deliver on that commitment. With these materials in front of you, start drafting your brand promise with a guarantee:

1. At a leadership team meeting—break your leadership team into groups of two.

2. Have each group review the work that has been completed to this date with a specific focus on your Core Customer's *needs*, not wants.

3. Have each group draft three brand promises with a guarantee. I am not a fan of just a brand promise—but if the groups can only come up with a brand promise for now, this is okay as this is a brainstorming stage.

4. Once each group has up to three brand promises with a guarantee to share—have each group present their ideas and post them on the whiteboard or easel paper.

5. Group together the ideas that are similar.

6. When all the groups have presented their ideas for a brand promise with a guarantee, have a discussion with the team to choose the top three brand promises with a guarantee.

7. Leave these promises in draft form for now and look for a few volunteers who will take these promises with a guarantee—very, very quietly—to test them on a few very friendly, existing Core Customers. See which ones have an impact based on the feedback received. You must test a brand promise with a guarantee before splashing it everywhere.

8. Repeat this process until you have a brand promise with a guarantee that the whole team agrees to. And by agreeing, I mean that the team knows it matters to the Core Customer and the team knows how to execute and measure success with the brand promise with a guarantee.

This will truly be a brainstorm exercise with the leadership team, as brand promises need time to percolate. When you can answer yes to the following questions, you'll know that you've got your unique brand promise:

- Does the brand promise with a guarantee attract customers to buy?

- Do your competitors think you're crazy to promise this with a guarantee to your customers?

- Does the brand promise matter to your Core Customer?

- Does the brand promise instantly differentiate your company in the marketplace?

Right, wrong, or ugly, go ahead and add your draft brand promise to your 3HAG. Don't leave that space blank; instead, gut it out. This will drive everyone in the whole company to comment, discuss, and evolve the idea into the best brand promise for your company.

The brand promise with a guarantee is the test that determines whether you've aligned your strategy, your 3HAG, correctly. In my experience of providing strategic growth business advice and coaching, I've discovered that a team might be totally committed to completing all the strategic work up to this point and have the Market Map, the Attribution Framework, mapping the Core Customer, and so on, but the key test to all this 3HAG work is how you have captured it in your brand promise with a guarantee. When you put it out into the marketplace, does your Core Customer respond positively? This is how we know we nailed it for today and will evolve it for the future.

Generally, a failing brand promise makes itself known right away and should force you to go back and look at your Core Customer and all the Strategic Pictures that you and your team have created to date, to see what you missed. Your brand promise should confirm your strategy, your 3HAG.

While it can be demoralizing when your brand promise doesn't connect with your Core Customers, it forces your team to come back and rework the strategy. Think of this as a gift and a way to save investment. Keep evolving, keep testing. The brand promise with a guarantee helps us to build confidence that we are investing time and resources in the right direction. If something isn't aligning, now is the time to figure out what's wrong and correct it.

Here are a couple of guiding questions to keep in mind if your brand promise isn't working:

- Are you promising something you can't achieve?

- Are you promising something that does not matter to the Core Customer, something you thought was an important need?

- Did you skip any of the strategic steps leading up to this point? If so, why? (Then go back and complete them!)

When you've figured out where your company can fill a void that really matters to your Core Customer, and where you can really deliver, you've found your unique brand promise. And once you've determined what your catalytic mechanism is, it becomes a matter of delivery. As we did at Subserveo, you'll need to empower your team to do whatever it takes to serve your Core Customer at all times.

Your Secret Sauce

As you learned in chapter 6, there's no reason to keep your strategy a secret. But there is one thing that should be a secret within your company, something that never gets shared or revealed to competitors: your Secret Sauce.

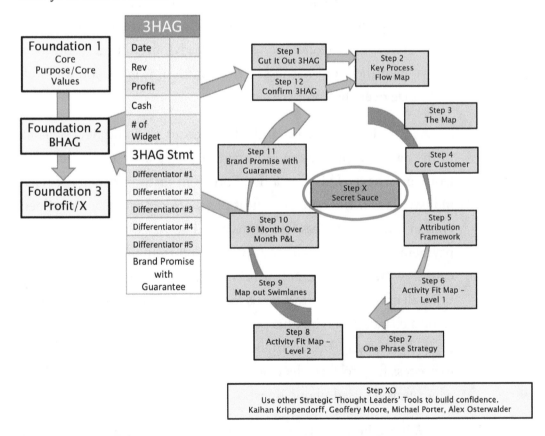

Your Secret Sauce is the unique solution to a problem in your industry that no one wants to solve. If you can devise a Secret Sauce for your company, you'll gain a significant edge over the competition because you will have identified a problem your customers face, or the market faces, and you'll have figured out how to address it when no else has figured it out, or does not want to solve it, or does not have the capability to solve it. If this sounds hard, you're right—it is. But you and your team should devote some time and resources to uncovering your market's Secret Sauce. As a CEO coach, I work with clients to identify their current Secret Sauce. Then we are also constantly looking for the next advantage, so that we're ready to evolve as required. This fits in great with our ever-evolving 3HAG. Keeping our 3HAG in focus helps us to keep our Secret Sauce in focus.

Verne Harnish calls the Secret Sauce the "X-Factor." It's your unique solution to an industry bottleneck, and it's difficult to discover. If it were easy, someone else would already have found it. But once you've identified and harnessed this solution, it gives you a tenfold advantage over the competition.

At Paradata, my team and I figured out that the Secret Sauce in the payment-processing industry was being able to map any data from anywhere. This was a huge problem in the financial services industry, as all the data specifications were proprietary and siloed. And in order to process face-to-face and non-face-to-face electronic payment transactions—in any country and from any country to any country—over the internet, we needed to solve this problem. At the time, all of our competitors let us forge ahead. They thought we didn't stand a chance at solving this problem. Actually, most people laughed at us. This was 1997, and their rationale was, who would ever want to process face-to-face electronic payments over the internet? That's why everyone used phone lines!

Well, we believed that was where the market was heading—that every business would eventually be plugged into the web and that using the internet to process face-to-face and non-face-to-face transactions would become the standard. It sounds obvious today, but this was radical thinking in the nineties.

We provided online payment-processing services for those businesses equipped to utilize them, while we also continued to process payments with other customers face-to-face. In other words, we already had the infrastructure in place for whenever our customers were ready to make the switch. In that sense, our Secret Sauce was being prepared for the internet before our customers—and certainly before our competitors—were. This Secret Sauce made us very valuable to others who believed the internet would play a critical role in payment processing.

By the time we sold Paradata, we had become the global leader in face-to-face and non-face-to-face electronic payment-processing services over the internet. We could map "any data from anywhere." That's the Secret Sauce difference.

When You Have a Secret Sauce but No Strategy: The Tale of Blockbuster

Blockbuster doesn't exist anymore, but once upon a time it was the largest chain of movie and video-game rental stores in the country. Initially Blockbuster's strategy was to leapfrog all the mom-and-pop corner video stores through a pioneering revenue-sharing arrangement with the major movie studios. That meant that Blockbuster would obtain videos for a tenth of the price that anyone else could. In return, the studios received some royalties on the back end.

This arrangement ensured that each Blockbuster franchise would have multiple copies of new-release movies and could rent them for far less than their competitors. In this way, Blockbuster became a massive company in a short time. Unfortunately, though, Blockbuster thought this was the only Secret Sauce it would ever need.

Depending on your age, you probably remember Friday night trips to the local Blockbuster for the evening's entertainment. The place was always hopping; the whole town was probably there. Everyone was making it a Blockbuster night. There were more than 8,000 Blockbuster stores in America at the company's zenith in 2004. Blockbuster was raking in the cash.

Then what happened?

By 2010 the company had filed for bankruptcy protection, because Netflix, and digital streaming, had come along. Yet it wasn't as though Netflix fell out of the sky and obliterated Blockbuster in a single cosmic explosion. Before Netflix got into digital streaming, it was in the mail-order DVD-rental business. Customers selected their titles on the company's website and then received a red envelope with their movies. You watched the DVDs, and then you mailed them back.

Blockbuster executives knew Netflix existed, but they didn't pay any attention to the start-up. They allowed Netflix to grow. What's more, Blockbuster was oblivious to the changes afoot in the video rental marketplace: the digital streaming revolution.

What's most astonishing is that Blockbuster *had* the infrastructure to get on that train—and not only to get on that train, but to *drive* that train. Instead, they didn't even see the forthcoming changes in the marketplace. Blockbuster's then-CEO John Antioco even had an opportunity to purchase Netflix in 2005. Netflix cofounder Reed Hastings offered his company to Antioco for $50 million. Since Antioco and his team didn't see where the industry was heading, they declined. They declined because they lacked a forward-looking strategy; they were unwilling to let an aging business model evolve for the twenty-first century.[5]

---

5 Celena Chong, "Blockbuster's CEO Once Passed Up a Chance to Buy Netflix for Only $50 Million," Tech Insider, *Business Insider*, July 17, 2015, http://www.businessinsider.com/blockbuster-ceo-passed-up-chance-to-buy-netflix-for-50-million-2015-7.

Blockbuster lost $1.1 billion in 2010, the year it filed for bankruptcy, while the company's valuation was just $24 million. That same year, Netflix had a growth spurt of $13 billion in value.

Blockbuster truly believed digital streaming didn't have a leg to stand on, that it was going to be a passing fad. Put another way, Blockbuster failed to recognize the biggest problem they needed to solve in order to remain relevant and gain an advantage in the marketplace: their Secret Sauce. Not the Secret Sauce that they had been nursing for decades, but the next Secret Sauce.

You and your team should never stop looking for the next Secret Sauce.

Netflix has continued to evolve, eyeing new developments in the industry. Today the company is focusing on two ingredients to its Secret Sauce: ultra HD streaming and producing original content to cater to its fragmented subscription base.[6]

The point is, Blockbuster got lazy, and its strategy was not focused on the future. Its team leaders needed to constantly examine the marketplace, analyze their internal operations, analyze the dimension they were on in contrast to industry competitors, and look ahead to deal with market and innovation changes coming down the pike.

Learn from Blockbuster's mistake: Don't get caught fat and flat-footed. It may cost you your company.

And your Secret Sauce is your underlying advantage. It's the unique solution that you bring to a problem facing your Core Customers. It gives your company a strategic edge, strengthening and solidifying your position in the marketplace. Never stop evolving it!

---

6 Dave James, "What's Next for Netflix's Streaming Tech?" News, *TechRadar*, August 29, 2015, http://www.techradar.com/news/television/what-s-next-for-netflix-s-streaming-tech-1300135.

Okay, So What's *Your* Secret Sauce?

This may take your team months or even years to figure out—or you may already know it (maybe the Secret Sauce in your industry is simple, even as none of your competitors are offering it). Regardless, identifying your Secret Sauce should be a high priority for your company. Start working on it immediately, and develop a rhythm (as with all other planning tools in this book) so that your team is regularly searching for your Secret Sauce—or your *next* Secret Sauce.

Here are a few ways you and your team can determine your Secret Sauce:

- **First of all, make it a priority.** Start looking for your Secret Sauce immediately. Remember, once you've found it, it gives you a tenfold advantage! It's well worth the effort it takes to discover it in the first place.

- **Look externally at your industry.** Where are the weak spots and pain points in this industry from the perspective of your Core Customer? Look at your industry's last few conference agendas—especially the breakout sessions—this is where some key issues that need to be solved in your industry come from. They're a great place to start identifying problems that are hard to solve in the industry.

- **Look internally at your own processes.** Where could your company improve its product line, delivery, timing, customer service, payment model, etc.?

- **At each meeting, move the conversation forward.** Be externally focused: Ask questions, test assumptions, discard ideas. And be internally focused: Ask questions, test assumptions, discard ideas. Continue this process until *you've found your Secret Sauce!*

- **Then repeat: Start looking for your next Secret Sauce.** Don't get caught asleep at the wheel like Blockbuster did. Other companies will eventually figure out your Secret Sauce, so you'll need a new one—and the sooner you start thinking about it, the better positioned you'll be to stay a step ahead of the competition.

If you're fortunate enough to figure out your Secret Sauce quickly, implement it as soon as possible. And if it takes you and your team months or even years to discern it, don't be discouraged. Be willing to talk about Secret Sauce at every strategy meeting. The continued discussion and focus will help you discover your Secret Sauce—your tenfold advantage.

Should You Share Your Secret Sauce?

NO!

NO!

NO!

This is your *Secret* sauce, not your *shared* sauce. Once you've discovered your Secret Sauce, keep it confidential. Letting competitors know your strategy is one thing; sharing your Secret Sauce is not recommended. If (and when) your competitors figure out what your Secret Sauce is—as happened with Blockbuster and many other successful businesses—don't stop looking for the next Secret Sauce That way, you will always be a step ahead—exactly where you want to be.

This will keep your company's 3HAG relevant as the market continues to evolve and your company evolves. This will be the topic of the next chapter—evolving your strategy, your 3HAG.

Check-in

1. Gut out your first 3HAG ✓
2. Create your Key Process Flow Map ✓

3.   Create your Market Map ✓

4.   Define your Core Customer ✓

5.   Create your Attribution Map ✓

6.   Name your 3–5 Differentiating Actions by completing your Activity Fit Map ✓

7.   Draw your Activity Fit Map II ✓

8.   Summarize your One-Phrase Strategy ✓

9.   Gut out your Swimlanes ✓

10. Create your 36 Month, month-over-month Rolling Forecast ✓

11. Determine your Brand Promise with a Guarantee and your Secret Sauce ✓

12. Create your 3HAG Checklist

13. Set your 3HAG Metronome

14. Confirm your Hedgehog Concept

CHAPTER TAKEAWAYS

✔ A *unique brand promise* addresses what you and your team believe is the greatest need your customers have and assures those customers that you can solve that problem better than any of your competitors.

✔ A brand *guarantee*, or "hurt," is how you make your brand promise hurt by, for instance, guaranteeing a refund if a customer is not completely satisfied. This will hurt your company unless you deliver reliable customer satisfaction. The guarantee is also known as a "catalytic mechanism," which forms a vital link between your company's goals and your actual performance.

✔ Your Secret Sauce is the unique solution to a problem in your industry that no one wants to solve—but you have the answer.

Finding your company's Secret Sauce may take years, but having one will give you a tenfold advantage over your competitors.

✔ Once you have your Secret Sauce, you can't sit back and get complacent—unless you want to end up like Blockbuster. Your team should always be looking for the *next* Secret Sauce.

Chapter 10

Evolve It!

Execution is the ability to mesh strategy with reality, align people with goals, and achieve the promised results.
—Larry Bossidy

ongratulations! You now have a full 3HAG. You have done the hard work of creating your short-, medium-, and long-term plans. You and your team now have clarity on *why* and *how* your company is going to achieve its three-year goal. You should be able to stand up and confidently state your strategy in a way that is aligned to your company's Core Purpose, your BHAG, and your twelve-month plan. Now let's evolve it and continue to build confidence.

We know that no strategy is static; in the business world, everything is draft. Yet you have taken the hardest step by creating your first 3HAG. Now we need to put in place a rhythm with your team so that you will forever evolve it.

Using a 3HAG is a continuous, never-ending process. On the 3HAG checklist below, there's a big white space for each of the tools to help you plan your next 3HAG movements as your 3HAG evolves. As a CEO and a CEO coach, I use this sheet to write down what we need to do next, how confident I am in what has been done, and where we should focus over the next three to four quarters with the team. This

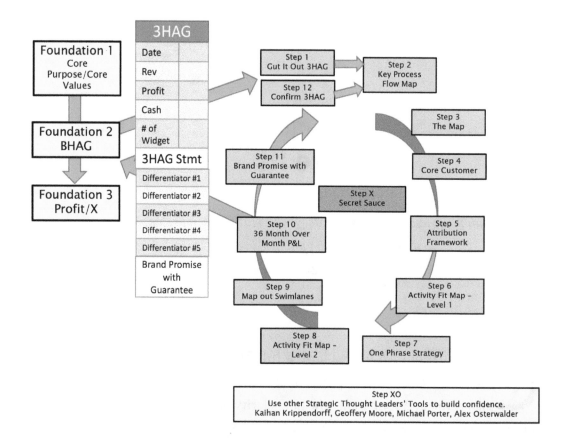

is also great for the leadership team to use, checking off tasks as you complete them and making notes on what you should revisit and when.

At Paradata, we had a war room in which the walls were covered with all the Strategic Pictures that we had created by using this framework, including our core values, Core Purpose, BHAG, and 3HAG. We were starting to feel the confidence of having our goals spelled out and a road map for how we were going to achieve those goals. We found ourselves having energized conversations about where we were going to be in one year, three years, and ten-plus years!

To keep us focused on where we were going, and to be sure that we were executing on the right priorities on a daily basis, we developed the 3HAG Strategic Execution System Checklist. This checklist, shown above, was key to keeping my team on track as we marched toward

3HAG – STRATEGIC EXECUTION SYSTEM - CHECKLIST

3HAG (3 Year Highly Achievable Goal)		Company:_____Year Ending:_____
Revenue		3HAG (3 Years)
Expenses		
Profit		
Cash		
The Map (External)		Key Process Flow Map (Internal)
Core Customer		Attribution Framework
3–5 Differentiating Actions		One Phrase Strategy
Swimlanes for 12 Quarters		36-Month Rolling Forecast
Brand Promise with Guarantee		Secret Sauce – 10x Advantage
Profit/X		BHAG (10–30 Year)

our 3HAG. (And now, as a coach, I use it to keep all my clients on track as they march confidently toward *their* 3HAGs.) This checklist can be used with your team to keep you focused as you work through the 3HAG framework presented in this book.

This checklist serves at least two purposes. It keeps the team focused on the right priorities in order to continue marching confidently forward, thereby keeping you from getting distracted, reverting to old habits, and reacting to competitors. But that's not all. The checklist also keeps you focused on the process itself. And the process is what builds confidence.

At Subserveo we kept our 3HAG checklist on the wall in our war room and used red, yellow, and green sticky notes to track our progress and our confidence on each of the components—and of course, overall—on our journey to a predictable and executable 3HAG. I hope you'll do the same: use the 3HAG checklist to show what is left to do, what you are confident in, and what you need to focus on to drive forward with clarity and confidence.

The way to get better at predicting the future is to continue this process and never stop evolving your strategy—your 3HAG.

How to Evolve It?

Throughout this book I have said that you and your leaders—your team—should meet and discuss each component from the 3HAG framework. A lot of companies ask how to find the time to stay focused on discussing the 3HAG. It's all about setting your company's "metronome." For more detailed information—check out my first book—*The Metronome Effect: The Journey to Predictable Profit*. Below we will focus on the rhythm set as well as what components of the 3HAG framework should be discussed and when.

We set out a meeting rhythm for the whole company. It was not about the meetings as much as it was about what we would discuss at each meeting and on what frequency. This allowed our team to stay focused by prebooking or preplanning our growth framework. It made sure that all the right people were prepared and involved in our company decisions. I will explain this at the end of this book so as to not overwhelm you with this communication and planning schedule.

Before you can outline your growth plan, you must set your Strategic Execution System rhythm with your team. We learned this rhythm from Verne Harnish's *Mastering the Rockefeller Habits*.[1] It's all about making sure the team is meeting at regular intervals so the whole company is making better and faster decisions aligned to their 3HAG and BHAG.

---

1 Verne Harnish, *Mastering the Rockefeller Habits* (New York: SelectBooks, 2006).

If that sounds like overkill, think of an Olympic soccer team. The team plans for the Olympics by training out on the field every day for four years. But before they even get out on the field, the coach creates a training and playing road map that covers each month, each quarter, each year all the way to the Olympic games. That's their 3HAG.

The same goes for running a business. What I've learned from coaching hundreds of businesses is that most companies don't take the time to set their company planning rhythm; they don't lay the right groundwork to ensure a successful growth planning process. And that's why I'm including the communication rhythm instructions. It's essential that you plan exactly when and how you and your team are going to gather to hammer out your company's plan, including your 3HAG. This is an important step for achieving your 3HAG.

So, how do you set your company's metronome?

- **Maintain a daily, weekly, monthly, quarterly, and annual meeting rhythm.** Each type of meeting requires a specific rhythm so that participants know what to expect and everyone stays focused. Below is a chart that shows what kind of rhythm works best for various types of strategy meetings. (For a detailed breakdown of why these types of meetings last for as long as they do, see chapter 8 of *The Metronome Effect*.)

- **Use the Outlook or Google calendar program to create a meeting invitation and have it repeat ad infinitum.** Look at your calendar and pick a date that works for everyone on your team, then send invitations. There is no excuse for not being able to find a common block of time where everyone can come together and talk about your company strategy. Reserve a conference room in advance as well.

The rhythm is important, but what is talked about in the meeting is even more important. Every meeting in the communication rhythm

Timing	Purpose/Type	Who	How Long?
2 Day Kickoff	Create/Confirm BHAG, 3HAG and create 1HAG for the company's goals. This meeting is held at the beginning of implementation.	Leadership Team	2 days
Communication Rhythm **Set Your Metronome**			
Daily	Connect Meeting—stay focused on company goals.	Leadership Team	15 min or less
Weekly	Tactical Execution Meeting—stay focus on company goals.	Leadership Team	1 hour or less
Weekly	Email from CEO to keep the team focused and accountable to the company goals.	Whole Company received email.	1 Page
Monthly	Confirm and/or evolve 3HAG/90 Day execution goals.	Leadership Team	4-8 hours
Monthly	36 Month Rolling Forecast Review with a focus on 1HAG/Annual Plan	Leadership Team	1 hour
Monthly	All Hands Meeting to keep the company focused on the company goals.	Whole Company	1 hour or less
Quarterly	Confirm and/or evolve BHAG, 3HAG and 1HAG based on analysis—create next 90-day plan for the company.	Leadership Team	8 hours
Annual	Confirm BHAG, evolve 3HAG and create 1HAG for the company's goals.	Leadership Team	2 days

has a standing agenda—meaning the agenda never changes, but what is talked about in each agenda item at every meeting is dynamic. Knowing what the agenda is at every meeting makes preparing your contribution to the meeting easier. Standing agendas are critical to ensure that meetings start and end on time, valuable decisions are made, and you and your team will meet your objectives. We all know poorly planned meetings can easily devolve into time-sucks. But if you've planned ahead and everyone is on the same page, these meetings will become dynamic, lively, productive gatherings that will give your company a strategic edge over your competitors.

Determine exactly what each meeting will cover and make sure attendees know the standing agenda for each meeting so they can come prepared. Then stick to that agenda. Happily, the agenda for each of these planning meetings has been set by best practices. Here's a sample agenda for an annual strategy meeting. (Download additional materials on standing agendas at http://www.shannonsusko.com.)

Annual	Strategy Execution	Leadership Team	2 Day Offsite
Prep	**Agenda – Day 1**	**Agenda – Day 2**	**Post**
☐ Functional Org. Review ☐ KPFM ☐ The Map ☐ SWOT ☐ Team Priorities Created ☐ A Player Review ☐ Metrics ☐ Plan Status Known ☐ Customer Feedback ☐ Team Feedback ☐ All Strategic Pictures Up on the Meeting Walls	• Good News • Objectives • Cohesive Team Work • Function Review • KPFM Review • Cultural System: Core Values, Core Purpose, BHAG • The Map Review • Strategy System: 3HAG • Wrap Up • One Phrase Close	• Good news • Objectives • Cohesive Team Work • Confirm 3HAG • SWOT • Annual Priorities • 90 Day Priorities • Individual Priorities • Critical Numbers • Wrap Up • One Phrase Close	☐ Leaders meet with their team to confirm plan. ☐ Leaders confirm priorities. ☐ Leaders share plan for Buy In. ☐ 12 Month Forecast is confirmed and aligned to plan. ☐ Leadership team meets before the year begins to lock in plan. ☐ Approval from Board.
		Tips And Benefits	
☐ All Leaders should meet with their teams prior to the meeting. ☐ All team members feel included. ☐ Feedback and ideas from the whole team.	☐ This is a Strategy day. ☐ All Strategic Pictures should be up on the wall and brought up to date. ☐ Your Core Customer should be at the table – picture of Cut Out.	☐ This is Execution day aligned to your 3HAG. ☐ Ensure the priorities are specific, measurable and owned. ☐ Ensure all understand the prioritization and alignment.	☐ Leaders needs to be able to share the Company Plan as good as the CEO. ☐ All teams involved to provide feedback. ☐ Townhall meetings is important for the kickoff and buy in.

The key to effective strategy execution sessions is to maintain a rhythm in your planning process. Once your team is accustomed to the rhythm of quarterly strategy meetings, you'll find that you plow through the agenda faster and with greater efficiency, as everyone will know to arrive prepared for the discussion. This gets easier and more exciting as this iterative habit becomes ingrained in your company culture.

Indeed, a habit like this is very powerful. Remember, 3HAG is *a repeatable Strategic Execution System*—repeatable all the way down to your meetings. Strategic planning is an ongoing process, a process of running one lap after another and getting stronger and more confident every time.

Evolve Meetings

Focus on the growth plan, including your 3HAG, in order to realize your company goals. Seems obvious—but it's harder to do in the reality of growing a company. As a CEO and now as a CEO coach, I carefully plan out what will be covered in what time frame according to where the company is in the implementation of the framework. I use the 3HAG checklist we discussed earlier to help keep this meeting plan on track.

On the next page is a sample plan and progression you can implement if you are just starting out with this framework.

This does not mean you don't hold your daily, weekly, or monthly meetings—they are imperative. But the table shows the progression of how to work through, quarter over quarter, getting better and better at your 3HAG; ensuring the analysis, discussion, and decisions are made; and staying focused on the BHAG and evolving the 3HAG as necessary. The alignment of the Strategic Execution System works well with the daily, weekly, and monthly meetings.

Powerful Strategic Pictures

Throughout this book we have talked about Strategic Pictures. I've always been a visual learner, and chances are most of the people on your team are too—including you. Studies suggest that the brain can process images seen for as little as thirteen milliseconds.[2] Scientists have confirmed that more than 80 percent of people are visual learners and that humans process visual images 600,000 times faster than we can read text.

Strategic Pictures create the story of your organization. Every component of the 3HAG framework is a picture that makes up your

---

2 Anne Trafton, "In the Blink of an Eye: MIT Neuroscientists Find the Brain Can Identify Images Seen for as Little as 13 Milliseconds," MIT News Office, MIT News, January 16, 2014, http://news.mit.edu/2014/in-the-blink-of-an-eye-0116.

The Strategic Execution System that Ensures Your Strategy Is Not a Wild-Ass-Guess!

R O = it → Forward

YEAR 1

Kick Off	Qtrly X	Qtrly X	Qtrly X
Function Review	Function Review	Function Review	Function Review
KPFM	KPFM	KPFM	KPFM
Core Values	Core Values	Core Values	Core Values
Core Purpose	Core Purpose	Core Purpose	Core Purpose
BHAG	BHAG	BHAG	BHAG
The Map	The Map	The Map	The Map
Gut Out 3HAG	Core Customer	Core Customer	Core Customer
12 Month	Attribution Map	Attribution Map	Attribution Map
Corp 90 Day	3-5 Diff. Actions	Activity Fit Map – One Phrase Strategy	Activity Fit Map – One Phrase Strategy
Indv. 90 Day	Evolve 3HAG	Evolve 3HAG	Evolve 3HAG
	12 Month	Start Swimlanes	Start Swimlanes
	Corp 90 Day	Start 36 Month F/C	Start 36 Month F/C
	Indv. 90 Day	12 Month	12 Month
		Corp 90 Day	Corp 90 Day
		Indv. 90 Day	Indv. 90 Day

YEAR X

Annual	Qtrly X	Qtrly X	Qtrly X
Function Review	Function Review	Function Review	Function Review
KPFM	KPFM	KPFM	KPFM
Core Values	Core Values	Core Values	Core Values
Core Purpose	Core Purpose	Core Purpose	Core Purpose
BHAG	BHAG	BHAG	BHAG
The Map	The Map	The Map	The Map
Core Customer	Core Customer	Core Customer	Core Customer
Activity Fit Map – One Phrase Strategy	Activity Fit Map – One Phrase Strategy	Activity Fit Map – One Phrase Strategy	Activity Fit Map – One Phrase Strategy
Brand Promise / w Guarantee	Brand Promise / w Guarantee	Brand Promise / w Guarantee	Brand Promise / w Guarantee
Use a Thought leader tool to confirm strategy.	Use a Thought leader tool to confirm strategy.	Use a Thought leader tool to confirm strategy.	Use a Thought leader tool to confirm strategy.
Evolve 3HAG	Evolve 3HAG	Evolve 3HAG	Evolve 3HAG
Swimlanes	Swimlanes	Swimlanes	Swimlanes
36 Month F/C	36 Month F/C	36 Month F/C	36 Month F/C
12 Month	12 Month	12 Month	12 Month
Corp 90 Day	Corp 90 Day	Corp 90 Day	Corp 90 Day
Indv. 90 Day	Indv. 90 Day	Indv. 90 Day	Indv. 90 Day

company's story. When we create our 3 Year Highly Achievable Goal (3HAG), the story is told mostly through images, not words.

Used properly, Strategic Pictures are an efficient way to tell your story, remember the strategic story, and provide clarity to every member of your team. Even if you think you're not a visual learner, chances are, most of your team is. Creating Strategic Pictures will help ensure overall success with this strategy.

A Picture Is Worth at Least a Thousand Words

As my Paradata team and I got our Strategic Execution System in place, we shifted our strategic planning time away from eleventh-hour meetings and began scheduling meetings during regular business hours. We found that Strategic Pictures were an essential tool for making those meetings productive. These Strategic Pictures sped up the time spent with our external analysis and internal analysis so we could focus on evolving the strategy.

By the time we launched Subserveo, we could see our Strategic Execution System clearly because we'd spent the time capturing the Strategic Pictures of our business for the current environment. These pictures kept all of us on the same page so we were all focusing on the right things. As you can imagine, in a high-growth business, it is vital that we all tell the same story. I have found that pictures are key in achieving this.

At Paradata and Subserveo, Strategic Pictures were always in front of us, at every meeting. When we shared pictures as a team, people could tell right away what we were talking about. They could see whether something had changed, internally or externally, since the previous meeting.

We never had to re-create the Strategic Pictures from scratch because we were always evolving them as required. This made it easier for everyone to participate in the discussion in a meaningful, productive way. It can be challenging for someone to articulate a strategy in words, and Strategic Pictures help make that articulation possible.

Also, it may take you five to ten minutes to explain your strategy to your team. Why spend that precious time on explanations when you've got a picture right in front of you that does all the explaining you need?

The stories around the pictures really help you build confidence in succinctly articulating your strategy to the whole company. Strategic Pictures *save you time*, build confidence, and allow your company to be nimble and to evolve as required. Strategy is not static, so the pictures are not, either.

Sometimes, I'll ask CEOs at my workshops to draw pictures for homework, and they'll come back the next day with a five-page explanation that probably took them an hour or two to crank out! To illustrate how Strategic Pictures can save time, I'll read their paper—and then draw a picture in about ten minutes that captures everything they so painstakingly wrote.

Tacking a picture on a wall is easier to do than photocopying a ten-page paper and passing it out, and most probably won't read it. Strategic Pictures are always there. When someone looks up, they're looking at your company's strategy—a physical reminder of your team's 1 Year and 3 Year Highly Achievable Goals.

Every tool in this book is a picture. Some pictures are simple, some are more complicated, but most can be drawn using boxes, lines, circles, and sometimes sticky notes.

The 3HAG Strategic Execution System Checklist is an overview of the many Strategic Pictures that will bring clarity to you and your team while they bring the end goal ever closer. Every step in the 3HAG is a picture: the Market Map, the Key Process Flow Map, the Core Customer, the Attribution Framework, 3–5 Differentiating Actions, One-Phrase Strategy, the Activity Fit Map—all those items and more can be represented by pictures.

The Strategic Pictures that you have been creating in every step of this framework are key to ensuring that meetings stay focused and, most importantly, efficient. The fact that these pictures are on your wall means that you do not have to go looking for them; they are easy to evolve on the fly of the meeting you are in and they keep everybody on the same page—same Strategic Picture—same strategic story—same 3HAG.

Many leadership teams wonder how we are going to cover all this ground laid out in the agendas of our meetings—especially the quarterly and annual meetings. These strategic meetings are kept on track by the Strategic Pictures. The Strategic Pictures are nothing fancy—I recommend that you do not make them fancy; keep them in original form—so it's easier to evolve them.

A 3HAG is a *Strategic Execution System* that drives confidence in predicting the future growth of your company *and* the framework to make it happen. The regular review and evolution of the 3HAG is what ensures that your company will take its short-term 1HAG/Annual Plan and confirm that it aligns with the BHAG. Companies ask me after many quarters of working through this framework, "What do we do when we get it completed?" Your 3HAG will never be complete due to the fact that time is moving forward, your market is changing around you, and your company is continually changing. So, based on the fundamentals of many business thought leaders of our time, the steps and components outlined above are key to keeping you and your company moving forward.

We used many tools to support and evolve our strategic thinking and are still adding more tools today as they make sense and become

3HAG: Strategic Execution System

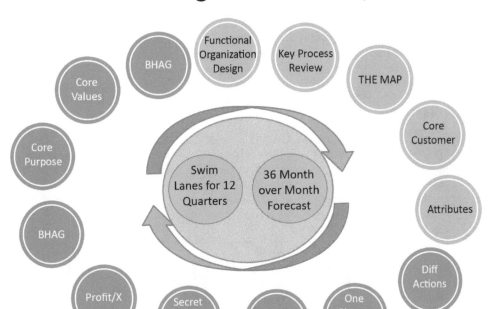

available for our newest business thought leaders. Next page are some of the other tools we have used to increase our confidence or evolve our 3HAG.

I use these tools often with my clients as we continue to focus quarterly on their strategy and 3HAG. Never stop looking for great tools to build your confidence and evolve your thinking.

First Next Step—Confirm Your Growth Foundation

Now that we have worked through all the key elements of your 3HAG, we are back at the foundation, where we started. In *Good to Great*, Collins explains the "Hedgehog Concept," which was inspired by a parable attributed to the ancient Greek poet Archilochus: "A fox knows many things, but a hedgehog knows one important thing."

Strategic Tool	Purpose	Thought Leader	Book Title
4th Option	This is a great tool to use if you are stuck on how to evolve your strategy, your 3HAG. I use this with leaderships regularly. This is a good approach to get the team thinking differently. I also love the questions to get the team thinking about the long term (BHAG) and the near term (3HAG). Aligns excellently with the 3HAG framework.	Kaihan Krippendorff	Outthink the Competition
Porter's 5 Forces	This tool is great to further your external analysis of the marketplace and get more visibility on your industry. This is a tool that I recommend once created to review at minimum every quarter through the strategic picture created with this tool.	Michael E. Porter	Competitive Strategy
Business Model Canvas	A tool to design, challenge, and evolve your business model. This is a visual tool that will become a strategic picture. This tool validates visually your business model and is a great complement to The Map.	Alexander Osterwalder	Business Model Canvas
Value Proposition Map	Develop products and services that customers want to buy. This is a great visual tool to support your Core Customer Description. This will bring your Core Customer to life even more. This will become a strategic picture for your wall.	Alexander Osterwalder	Value Proposition Design
Position Statement	Craft a short, effective "elevator pitch" that states your core customer, the problem you're solving, your product, and how it uniquely solves a problem in your market space. This is a great tool to get the whole team describing your company the same way.	Geoffrey Moore	Crossing the Chasm
Value Proposition Statement	Craft a short, effective value proposition that should pull together all your 3HAG work in one succinct sentence that has impact to your audience.	Geoffrey Moore	Crossing the Chasm

Note: All of these tools can be found at shannonsusko.com.

This idea became a business mantra in 1953, when British philosopher Isaiah Berlin built on the idea by dividing famous writers and thinkers into two categories: hedgehogs and foxes. Hedgehogs look at the world with a single, defining idea. Plato and Proust were hedgehogs.

Foxes, as exemplified (according to Berlin) by Aristotle and Shakespeare, cannot boil the world down to a single concept or idea.

Collins took this a step further and applied it to business leaders. Rather than pursuing many goals at the same time and thereby risking unfocused attention, hedgehog organizations focus on one thing—and though they may be slow, they outmaneuver the foxes. In a battle for survival, the hedgehog generally wins, no matter how sneaky the fox may be.

To outperform your competitors, you and your team must adopt a hedgehog mentality by devoting your energy, talent, and resources to the *one thing* you can be best at in the world.

I like to work with teams at this point in time to reconfirm and get clearer on the Foundation for Growth. With your leadership team, consider each of the following:

1. Hand out pads of sticky notes and markers to each leader.

2. **Understand your company's passion.**

   Ask the question, "What inspires you and your team to come to work every day?" and get each leader to write down their answer on a sticky note. This question is reframing the original question about your Core Purpose: "Why does your company exist?" We are looking for consistency regarding the original answer or we need to evolve our answer for clarity and alignment. Get each leader to share their answer from the sticky note and put it up in front of the team for discussion and confirmation.

3. **Understand how your team succeeds and how it doesn't.**

   This step requires total honesty. Be realistic about what your team is good at and where you could improve. If you're focusing on something other than your core business, you're not acting like a hedgehog! Focus instead on what your company can be *best at in the world*. Ask the following question: "What can the company be best at in the world?" Get each leader to write down their answer on a sticky note and then share it with the rest of the leadership team. Group the common answers together and then discuss as a team what it is you can be best at in the world. Remember this is not a goal or a plan but an understanding of what you can be best at.

4. **Understand your economic engine (Profit/X).**

Everything in this book is designed to set your company apart from your competitors. The Profit/X tool determines whether your 3HAG and your BHAG are in alignment. Another way to think of your economic engine is as a key performance indicator (KPI): something that you and your team can point to that empirically shows improvement in your business. This is the way to measure your progress toward your 3HAG and BHAG.

As I mentioned all the way back in chapter 2, Jim Collins calls a company's KPI the "Profit/X." You drafted your Profit/X back when you did your first gutted-out 3HAG; now let's go a little deeper.

You and your team must understand how you generate sustained cash flow; this is your *economic engine*. In this book, we've already mapped out your Key Process Flow Map (KPFM), in which you named the three to five key processes/functions that make your company money. The KPFM allows you to see these key processes and how they flow to create widgets and generate cash. So go ahead and pull out the KPFM you drafted in chapter 4. Where does your company's cash flow come from, now and in the future? Does your company generate sustained cash flow via profit per product category, profit per user, or profit per transaction? (This is why the economic engine is called "profit per X!")

Let's once again go back to the example of Southwest Airlines. While most airlines would describe their economic engine as *profit per mile* or *profit per seat*, Southwest uses *profit per plane in the air*. Southwest makes money when the planes are flying. This economic engine drives Southwest's entire strategy.[3] Paradata's economic engine was *profit per merchant*, while Subserveo's was *profit per user*.

So what is your "X"? This is a confirmation question to test your earlier profit/X. Ask the following question: "What will our profit/X be?" Get each leader to write down their answer on a sticky note and then share it with the rest of the leadership team. Group the common answers together and then discuss so that you can come to agreement on what your profit/X will be at this time.

Once you've got your X, you have a clearer picture of how your company is making money right now and how it will make money in the future. You need your X in order to align your twelve-month plan with your 3HAG and your BHAG.

Your company should be able to forecast a number for your X for twelve months as well as by month and quarter, in each fiscal year of the 3HAG. This value should be confirmed and reflected in your 36 Month, month-over-month Rolling Forecast.

5. **Look for overlap: BHAG confirmation.**

Drawn out, the Hedgehog Concept looks like this:

---

3 Verne Harnish, "2 Critical Vision Decisions: Profit Per X and BHAG," *Gazelles*; 2013, page 4, https://gazelles.com/static/resources/articles/ProfitPerXBHAG.pdf.

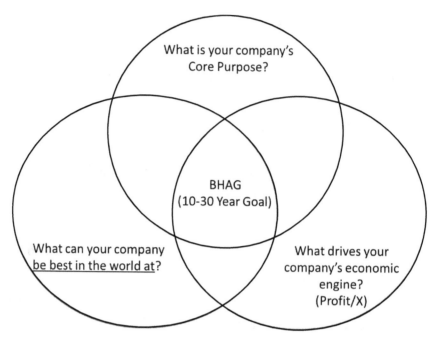

Adapted from Jim Collins's *Good to Great*

The region in the middle where these three components overlap is your BHAG. As a hedgehog, you want to stay focused on your BHAG and thereby outmaneuver the fox.

This analysis is a great way to come back around to your Foundation for Growth and become more confident about your BHAG.

Where Hedgehog Meets 3HAG

Back in chapter 1, we talked about your team getting on a bus and asking, "Where are we going?" Your BHAG is your answer to that question. The next thing they'll ask is, "How will we get there, and how long will it take?" The answer to those questions is, you guessed it, your 3HAG. And when the bus starts moving, your twelve-month execution plan kicks in. Instead of driving around the block, the bus heads straight toward your 3HAG, which is your route to your BHAG.

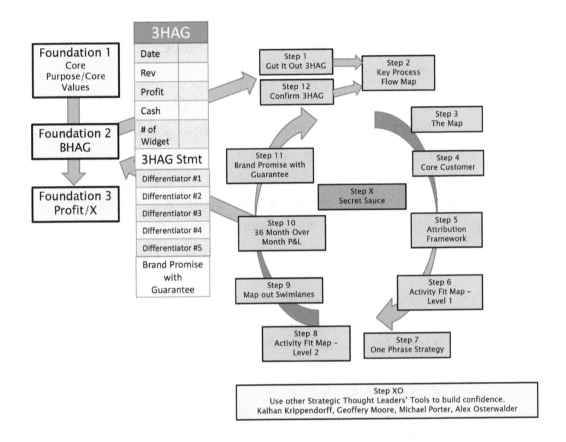

As a hedgehog—that is, as a company focused singularly on your BHAG, following your 3HAG in order to get there—you and your entire team now have clarity on where you're going and how you're getting there, quarter over quarter.

Track Your Progress

The 3HAG is a *Strategic Execution System*. This system melds your strategy and execution into one framework. You will meet regularly to discuss how you are progressing and in what direction you should head next. This is why we will create a communication rhythm to ensure that you know where you are at all times.

At Paradata and Subserveo, we implemented this framework using Strategic Pictures, which I highly recommend, and we used Word and

Excel documents to track our progress, which I do *not* recommend. This was all we had available to us at the time, and wanting to stay focused like a hedgehog, we did not create our own tool to track our progress.

When I became a CEO coach for high-growth teams, I could not imagine exposing the teams I work with to the Word and Excel templates we used to track our progress. They were inefficient and did not create the visible playing field we were looking for. So I created a tool with one of my former development team leads for use with my companies and for myself as a coach. In January 2006, we cofounded a company called Metronome Growth Systems with two of my former team members from Paradata and Subserveo. This platform allows all teams of any size to track their progress toward their BHAG, 3HAG, 1HAG/Annual Plan, and of course their ninety-day plan. This is a key tool for all teams to utilize to create the visibility required to make decisions faster, stay focused, and realize their team and individual goals. This platform drives team results, and it will decrease your risks and increase the Team Accountability we are coaching for as leaders. I am a little biased, as I am one of the creators of this platform, but the platform is used today by over a hundred coaches and their clients. (For more information, visit http://www.metronomegrowthsystems. com/.) No matter whether you use Metronome Growth Systems or another platform or Word or Excel—track your progress and share it often with your team.

In the final chapter, we'll explore strategies for execution, as well as the payoff from having a fully formed 3HAG. Congratulations on coming so far!

Check-in

1. Gut out your 3HAG ✓

2. Create your Key Process Flow Map ✓

3. Create your Market Map ✓

4. Define your Core Customer ✓

5. Create your Attribution Map ✓

6. Name your 3–5 Differentiating Actions by completing your Activity Fit Map ✓

7. Draw your Activity Fit Map II ✓

8. Gut out your Swimlanes ✓

9. Complete your 36 Month, month-over-month Rolling Forecast ✓

10. Determine your Brand Promise with a Guarantee and your Secret Sauce ✓

11. Create your 3HAG Checklist ✓

12. Set your 3HAG Metronome ✓

13. Confirm your Hedgehog Concept ✓

CHAPTER TAKEAWAYS

✔ How to set your metronome—your communication rhythm to stay focused, have fun, and march toward the freedom you are looking for.

✔ How to create your 3HAG checklist—and use it to stay focused and on track.

✔ How to develop quarterly meetings and your 3HAG progression—by implementing the 3HAG all at once. Once you have gone through the whole framework, refine it again to continue to increase your confidence.

✔ The Hedgehog Concept holds that a fox knows many things, but a hedgehog knows one important thing. Ultimately the hedgehog's single-mindedness will enable it to win out over the wily but scatterbrained fox. In business, the *one thing* your company should focus on, tuning out all the noise in the marketplace, is your BHAG. Your 3HAG, of course, is your road map to your BHAG, and the Hedgehog Concept is foundational to the 3HAG.

✔ Track your progress regularly and share it with the team. Use a tool like Metronome Growth Systems to track real-time progress to make quicker decisions.

Chapter 11

3HAG: Focus, Fun, and Freedom

If you are persistent, you will get it.
If you are consistent, you will keep it.
—Harvey Mackay

This chapter is all about how executing your 3HAG gives you focus—and ultimately freedom—and allows you to have fun along the way.

At this point in your 3HAG development, your team members have a clear view of how cash is or will be coming into the business and how decisions will be made for the future. With your 3HAG in hand, you and your team should feel a newfound confidence. You have a defined strategy for how you're going to carve out your unique and valuable position in your market, and you can clearly predict where your company will be in three years because you have a quarter-by-quarter road map. And as you grow more and more familiar with the 3HAG framework and continue to refine and evolve your 3HAG in response to external and internal factors, you will feel ever-greater confidence. Building that confidence is an iterative process that comes through using the 3HAG framework and methods on a consistent basis. That's the confidence loop.

It's also possible that you don't yet have a solid 3HAG and your team still has some work to do—and that's to be expected at this point. It doesn't matter how long it takes. I worked with one company recently whose team leaders mapped out their 3HAG and all their Strategic Pictures in two days. This is great, but it is extremely rare. The leaders at this company were so energized by the idea of having their strategy mapped out that they committed to gutting out the whole 3HAG in two days. (Even in this case, though, the team leaders took more time to complete their 36 Month Rolling Forecast.) This particular team wanted to get this material in front of everyone as soon as possible so they could move into the execution phase and start building confidence.

Conversely, I've seen companies take anywhere from four months to twenty-four months to work out a 36 Month Rolling Forecast, and that's okay, too. Remember, as long as you've got your draft 3HAG, it doesn't matter if it takes twenty-four hours or twenty-four months to finish it. Commit to spending the time on it together with your team, and you will succeed.

Of course, the truth is that your 3HAG is always a draft. That's the reality of the business world. Strategy creation is *always* in draft mode because the market you're playing in does not stand still. You will always be checking your position and adjusting.

The Rhythm of a Strategic Execution System

You now have a system in place to ensure that you and your team meet regularly to plan and review your progress. You might remember that the rhythm of your meeting schedule is one of the first things I discussed all the way back in chapter 1. I'm guessing you understand now why I would emphasize meeting schedules and agendas as such an important topic.

A 3HAG is no good if you don't act on it; your 3HAG may be the best thing since sliced bread, but it's just another piece of paper until you put it to work. Over the course of my career as a coach to CEOs, I've worked with plenty of team leaders who developed magnificent 3HAGs and communicated their objectives clearly and concisely with their teams, but then hit a roadblock when it came to action and accountability. Here, we're ensuring that your team commits to action by setting up a *rhythm of Team Accountability*. You and your team actively create that rhythm of Team Accountability when you establish regular weekly, monthly, quarterly, and annual strategic planning meetings. This is where you and you team will make better, faster decisions aligned with your 3HAG.

The great news is that when you create your 3HAG, you're not doing it alone—you're sharing it with your whole leadership team and beyond. By sharing your Strategic Execution System, you're sharing accountability—and shared accountability drives everyone to win. A complete 3HAG helps the team cohere, which in turn ensures their ability to execute the strategy. All these elements go hand in hand.

Indeed, by building a 3HAG, you're encouraging everyone on your team to trust you and to trust one another. Why? Because you've now defined what separates your company from your competitors in the marketplace. You know your unique and valuable position. You know exactly what steps you're going to take to achieve your 3HAG.

You've given yourself permission to work on things today to benefit your company in the future. And everyone on your team has the same permission because you've created your strategic plan together.

You've also built quarterly benchmarks along the way that incentivize your team to do well. Not only are you and your team able to celebrate your collective victories, but you can see the wins coming. That keeps everyone energized and looking toward the future.

You can think of all these daily, weekly, monthly, and quarterly meetings as practice for the big game. There will come a time when your company is seeking investment from private equity firms, or when you want to take your company public, or even exit. Creating the 3HAG is a leadership best practice; completing these Strategic Pictures and maps helps the leaders on your team build confidence for the long haul.

Have Fun Along the Way

My goal when working with business clients is twofold. First, create a viable, actionable growth plan tied together with the 3HAG. Second, have fun! It is actually possible to enjoy your work when you've got clarity about what you're doing and you've included the whole team. I experienced this with my own companies (after a rocky start!), and I've seen it happen again and again with my clients.

On the other side of the coin, working hundred-hour weeks, being constantly glued to your phone, and running from crisis to crisis is *not* effective strategic leadership. It's a recipe for burnout and low team morale. A solid 3HAG allows you and your team to work a normal week, have clarity and confidence about what you're doing, and be comfortable leaving work at the door when the day is done.

When I first launched Paradata, I was working seven days a week, one hundred hours a week, often long into the night. That wasn't sustainable, and it served neither the company nor me. After we developed the growth framework tied together with our 3HAG, our team developed a rhythm, and I started to feel confident enough to reestablish balance in my life.

Good thing, because four years into Paradata, I got married and had three kids in less than three years. Many of us find it challenging to be a good parent *and* a good steward of a company. The 3HAG framework makes that possible too. Thanks to our 3HAG, I knew we had created a differentiated strategy that would work whether I was in the office or not. Once we established a rhythm for ourselves, I trusted my team because I knew we were well enabled to execute that strategy.

You and your team have worked together to create a great 3HAG. If you didn't trust your team, you probably wouldn't have made it this far. Trusting your team means you understand that your company will do well even if you're not at the helm. By establishing a 3HAG, you've built a disciplined team that expects certain things to happen regularly—like rhythmic, consistent meetings and correct decisions. Now your company is gaining forward momentum because you've established accountability and trust among your team members, allowing you to find a balance between your work life and your personal life.

You've read this book. You've put these tools to work. And now you're going to reap the benefits of a better quality of life, a better-run company, and the goals you set out to achieve. That's no small deal.

Leaders Build Great Teams That Execute Great 3HAGs

Once Paradata was acquired, many of my former Paradata teammates actually wanted to come with me to build Subserveo. Why? Because they knew that we would create clear goals and an achievable road map from the very start. At Paradata, we had created a culture that rewarded cohesiveness, ownership of Team Goals, and acting on core values.

How many people on your team would follow you to a new company? The answer to that question tells you about the work environment and cohesion you've created. Don't worry; even if you don't think your team members would follow you today, you're still at the beginning of the 3HAG process—the process of building a great team to execute a great 3HAG.

3HAG Reduces Risk and Increases Value: Subserveo's Payoff

Your 3HAG spells out clear projections for where your company will be in three years. By nailing down those projections, you've effectively increased your company's value—because you've decreased risk.

A fully actionable 3HAG reduces risk no matter which side of the bargaining table you're on. If you're the purchaser, you know exactly how much risk you're assuming; if you represent the business being acquired, you've done all the hard work already—you and your team have discussed the bumps in the road and how you're going to address them. Rather than being *reactive*, your 3HAG ensures *proactive* thought and execution.

Now that you've got all the pieces figured out, standing in front of investors or board members won't cause you to break into a cold sweat. Now, when you're challenged about any aspect of your company, you have the resources to answer with confidence: *Yes*, we know what we're doing, where the company is going, and how we're going to get there, in detail.

You can now articulate your 3HAG in under a minute—and if you can't yet, then you soon will—because you know the unique and valuable position that you're going to carve out in the white space of your market. You have now established the discipline within your team to create a Strategic Execution System, and you have the confidence to share the 3HAG with whoever approaches you about it.

After we built Subserveo with some of my old Paradata teammates, it was only three years before a partner expressed interest in buying us out. Our due diligence in that process required that we send our "business plans" from the past three years. We didn't have a business plan for the previous three years, but we did have twelve pieces of paper that represented twelve quarters: three years of business planning in our One-Page Strategic Plan, quarter by quarter. That's what we sent. Providing those twelve pages was a turning point in negotiating the deal.

The twelve pages illustrated the path we executed to achieve our 3HAG. Page one stated where we were going to be in three years, while page twelve revealed that that was exactly what we had achieved. The acquirer saw that we'd been able to accurately predict, back in quarter one, where we would be in quarter twelve. The theoretical numbers matched up with what actually happened.

That realization changed the dialogue about the acquisition. The acquirer realized what we were really about; not only did we have something special and strategic, but our team knew how to accurately predict Subserveo's financial future and execute on it.

By showing the historical prediction and execution history of Subserveo, we had effectively increased our value by many more zeros than we ever thought we'd see.

Moving Forward

One thing always happens with every organization I've worked with: Team leaders find that they are no longer driving their company around the block. They now have the momentum to drive forward, toward their 3HAG and BHAG.

I've also worked with quite a few companies that overachieve, meaning they arrive at their 3HAG faster than they predicted they would. It makes sense: When you start mapping out in detail how your company will succeed, the enthusiasm and competitive drive start to kick in. You want to meet those goals, and maybe you want to meet them even sooner than you said you would.

If that happens to you—if you find that you meet your goals early—simply adjust those goals upward and continue your forward drive. This, of course, is the confidence you and your team are looking for.

Never stop evolving your 3HAG—your Strategic Execution System that will drive your predictable profit! Enjoy the focus, fun, and freedom. I wish you good luck and great 3HAGs all along the way!

Printed in the USA
CPSIA information can be obtained
at www.ICGtesting.com
LVHW081455121223
766150LV00019B/1697